Life

with

WAL-MART

A Vendor's Story

By Kunmi Oluleye

IROK Solutions, Inc.
Stone Mountain, Georgia

Published by: IROK Solutions, Inc.
4002 Highway 78, Suite 530-192
Snellville, Georgia 30039 U.S.A.
http://www.lifewithwalmart.com

Cataloging-in-Publication Data
Oluleye, Kunmi 1963-
Life with Wal-Mart.: A Vendor's Story/Kunmi Oluleye
p. cm.
Includes index
Library of Congress Control Number: 2007929355
ISBN 10: 0-9654-8013-5   ISBN 13: 978-0-9654801-3-0
1. Food Industry and trade – United States
2. Marketing -- United States
3. Strategy   4. Management

I. Oluleye, Kunmi   II. Title

HF5429.215.U6 F31   2007
381.149'15 – dc 22

http://www.lifewithwalmart.com

Printed in the United States of America
1   3   5   7   9   10   8   6   4   2

Contents

Acknowledgement

To my children for all you do.
Make this a point of reference of
God's Strength.
To Him be the Glory!

God will paralyze every

demon that resists

my progress in Jesus Name!
Amen

The speech below by Nelson Mandela was originally
written by Marianne Williamson. I personalized it.

*My deepest fear is not that I am inadequate. My
deepest fear is that I am powerful beyond measure. It is my
light, not my darkness, that frightens me most. I sometimes ask
myself, who am I to be brilliant, gorgeous, talented and
fabulous? Actually, who am I not to be?*

*I am a child of God. My playing small doesn't
serve the world. There's nothing enlightened about shrinking so
that other people won't feel insecure around me. I am meant
to shine. I am born to make manifest the Glory of God that
is within me. It's not just in some of us, it's in everyone.*

*As I let my light shine, I unconsciously give other
people permission to do the same. As I am liberated from
my own fear, my presence automatically liberates others.*

Say it out loud, daily!

ABOUT THE AUTHOR

Born in Lagos, Nigeria, Kunmi Oluleye, moved to the United States at the age of 14. She started cooking at the age of 8, not by choice, but because she is the oldest of four children and was in charge of the house while both parents pursued full time careers.

While growing up, her father owned and operated a bakery business and she was required to work when not doing homework or other chores. From the 1950s, her grandfather, Joshua Ade Tuyo, had a business in Nigeria called DeFacto Bakery and Eateries at Yaba, Lagos, Nigeria. It was famous throughout Nigeria and other parts of Africa, for its breads, cakes, meat-pies and sausage rolls. His establishment greatly influenced the baking industry in most of Africa. One could say that cooking is in the family.

Kunmi's undergraduate and graduate degrees are from Simmons College in Boston, Massachusetts. She has over 15 years of experience in these industries: Food, Technology, Consulting and Corporate Event Planning. As of July 2007, Kunmi's latest trade participation was in February 2007 with the USDA Trade Mission to Nairobi, Kenya, and AGOA Workshop with the West African Trade Hub, to Douala, Cameroun.

Kunmi is the author of two other books, *Selling My Food to Supermarkets, Distributors, Etc.*, a story of how an African woman crossed various barriers: cultural, race, gender, faith and issues of being a small business and *The*

Cure of Chronic Hepatitis B, a documentation of one man's cure of Hepatitis B with the Ribavirin and Interferon therapy.

Sheba Foods has been widely covered by media. To view TV clips, magazine articles and other news, please visit this webpage www.shebafoods.com/news.aspx. To have Kunmi as a speaker, more information available on the speaker page at www.shebafoods.com/speaker.aspx.

ABOUT THIS BOOK

This is a book that I almost did not publish. As a Wal-Mart supplier, I feel a need to share my Wal-Mart journey with everyone. I had the idea to write this book in March 2006, given all the hell that broke loose with Wal-Mart. There were so many distractions, discouraging comments and events. Every person I told about the book or read the manuscript has serious reservations and concern for my well being. What if the people I talk about, Ambassador Andrew Young and Mr. Jesse Jackson react negatively? What if Wal-Mart and Dun & Bradstreet have a temper tantrum? Can I deal with it? What if someone sues me for libel? What if other supermarkets blacklist me for fear that I might write about them? They may not approve my products or those products I represent regardless of quality and need. What if this? What if that? As I pondered all concerns, thoughts and suggestions, the only thing that kept coming to my mind was: What would Jesus do if he had my experience? He would definitely spread the word! I am simply following his footsteps.

It was difficult keeping emotions out of this book. I didn't want to be portrayed as an irate black woman lashing out at Wal-Mart or the others that I talk about. I hope that everyone mentioned takes this book constructively, so as to not allow what happened with our relationship to repeat itself. The questions posed to you throughout the book is for you to ponder points made. I tried to remain as objective as possible in stating the facts, to allow you to draw your own conclusions. Chapters Three to Five were the most difficult to write, with Chapter Five being the most excruciating. It forced me to revisit painful memories that

I'd rather have left alone. I hardly ever cry. Most people including my family call me the Iron Woman. A lot of the suppressed tears were shed during the Wal-Mart experience.

This book would be incomplete if I excluded my culture and religion, the basis of my foundation. I am Yoruba, a tribe in Nigeria. In different Chapters, I share Yoruba proverbs applied during the Wal-Mart experience. Even though I am a Christian, I have lost faith in the Church. The Christians I come in contact with can't seem to do right. Given the Halleluyahs and spiritual victories stated in the book, it would be misleading to not disclose that I have not been to Church in years, yet the Trinity shows up in full force when I call on Them. Psalm 116: 1-2 niv sums up my feelings about God. "I love the LORD, for he heard my voice; he heard my cry for mercy. Because he turned his ear to me, I will call on him as long as I live."

Recap of the reasons for writing this book.

- To share my Wal-Mart's two and a half year journey, so that potential and current suppliers will know how react if faced with similar situations.

- To challenge the African-Americans to buy African foods.

- To explore and engage conversation on what happens when Wal-Mart opens stores in Africa.

Visit the book's website http://www.lifewithwalmart.com for updates, questions or feedback.

Warning – Disclaimer

Chapter One

So you want to sell your product to Wal-Mart?

Where there's a WILL,
there are five hundred relatives.

I would like to start by stating that most of the time, the voice in the book is speaking to everyone. Occasionally, my voice fluctuates between speaking to the general public then to the potential Wal-Mart supplier.

It is true that a small company doing business with Wal-Mart can attain million dollar status overnight. That can come at the price of one's sanity. It is also true that the same company doing business with Wal-Mart can become bankrupt overnight in less time than it took to attain the million-dollar status. I kept in mind the riches to bankruptcy possibility. I did not make any major equipment or capital investment once approved as a supplier. For both the deli and freezer entries, I decided it best to hire a company with the appropriate setup to produce my products. Should the Wal-Mart business cease, I wouldn't be in a desperate position.

I am not saying to not sell to Wal-Mart, sales can be good and they paid me on time. I am saying to do your homework, get all the facts before making that decision. It is common knowledge that Wal-Mart will do whatever deal makes them money, including taking a product off the shelf, if approached with a similar one that is two cents less. In the Wal-Mart supplier agreement that I signed, it stated that Wal-Mart can pull my product off the shelf without notice and for no reason. Chapters Three to Five share the Sheba Foods' Wal-Mart ordeal, giving a glimpse of what suppliers are likely to encounter. Many people told me to guard against Wal-Mart duplicating my products and selling it cheaper. Given the uniqueness of the products and that the market had not been quantified, I had no worries of this happening.

Wal-Mart was started by a devote Christian. Founded on Christian principles with the intension of helping lower income people stretch their dollar. That they did well, while putting small businesses in surrounding areas out of business. This is one of the reasons why many protest Wal-Mart's entry into their communities, and are successful in blocking Wal-Mart from building stores in their cities. As Wal-Mart grew bigger, many of the Christian principles were lost in the process. I am Christian and consistently disappointed as to how Christians behave worse than non-believers. Wal-Mart is one example of my disappointment. I feel that those who distance themselves from Wal-Mart do it based on ethics. Usually, they object to the way Wal-Mart treats its workers and suppliers. I also feel that those who embrace Wal-Mart, embrace all of Wal-Mart's wrong doings for their personal gains.

DISTANCING FROM WAL-MART

There are many people and organizations that do not only distance themselves from Wal-Mart, they actively speak out against Wal-Mart. I read a *U.S. News* article published on May 23, 2007. Senator Barack Obama's wife quits as Director of TreeHouse Foods, a Wal-Mart supplier. Her husband has been one of the most outspoken critics of the retail chain in the Senate. My guess is that she decided it was time to publicly support her husband's stand in regards to Wal-Mart.

"Many companies do business with Wal-Mart," said Chris Kofinis, Communications Director for WakeUpWal-Mart.com, a project of the United Food and Commercial Workers union. "The difference is whether one stays silent on Wal-Mart`s negative business practices or not. Senator Obama has not stayed silent and he should be applauded for that." I found a wealth of Wal-Mart facts, dates and other details on the wakeupwalmart.com website. As I read the *U.S. News* article, I thanked God for the Obama family and all those who speak up, keeping pressure on Wal-Mart to change their business practices.

Another wonderful resource was Robert Greenwald's movie *Wal-Mart: The High Cost of Low Price* which spotlights Wal-Mart supplier and employee practices. I finally watched the movie in its totality July 2007. To my surprise, shoppers are not safe on Wal-Mart's property. I was stunned to see how many murders, rapes, abductions and other crimes occurred in the Wal-Mart parking lots, with Wal-Mart doing nothing about it. There are accounts of asking managers to lie, defiant of laws, destruction of the eco-system and much more. These are other reasons people use to block Wal-Mart's entry into their communities. Given statistics that 57% of U.S. Southerners shop at Wal-Mart, I was surprised to see two cities in Georgia, listed among those who successfully blocked Wal-Mart from building in their area. The movie was educative and may change your view about Wal-Mart. Everyone must watch this movie! To buy a DVD or get more information please visit www.walmartmovie.com. You may stop shopping at Wal-Mart after watching the movie. One way people distance themselves from Wal-Mart.

EMBRACING WAL-MART

Wal-Mart continues their business practices because there is not enough pressure on them to change. I believe that it will take more than my not shopping at Wal-Mart to effect the necessary change in its business practices. Prior to watching Robert Greenwald's movie, I shopped a lot at Wal-Mart. I felt I was supporting suppliers that Wal-Mart mistreats, while contributing to the job security of Wal-Mart's employees. Those in places of power are better able to get the necessary changes. It is a shame that many people who can speak up don't. Silence means consent. Those who embrace Wal-Mart help perpetuate their unethical business practices. During my ordeal with Wal-Mart, many of the resources I called upon did not respond because they benefited from Wal-Mart through through advertising, sponsorship or consultancy.

As a certified U.S. Women Business Enterprise, I wrote a letter to the President of the organization sharing my Wal-Mart experience. I requested that my experience be shared with other members so that they would be better prepared if planning on doing business with Wal-Mart. I got an email back stating the WBE organization (WBENC) cannot share my information with anyone. Wal-Mart sits on the board of the WBENC.

Then there was a man whose company is one of Wal-Mart's minority advertising agencies. He was a wonderful and sweet Christian Bible carrying man. He not only showed me the Bible he kept in his office, but the story on how he got it. He invited me to a high powered event were he was one of the main sponsors. Here he introduced me to Mr. Jesse Jackson. The advertising man committed to help with sponsorship for my Flavors of Africa event being hosted in Atlanta. As soon as I disclosed my problems with Wal-Mart, he stopped returning my phone calls. He would make appointments, only to cancel them. I stopped calling him. To be honest, I understood his business position. He could lose a major customer; but given the stories about his relationship with Jesus, I wondered about his Christian walk as he abandoned his Christian sister in distress.

I called Ambassador Andrew Young and Mr. Jesse Jackson's office numerous times. The Mr. Jackson referred to throughout this book is known by most people as Reverend Jesse Jackson. I sent letters asking for their help with the Wal-Mart issues. I received minimal response from Ambassador Young's office, no response from Mr. Jackson or his office. Mr. Jackson should not use the title Reverend. According to Kenneth Timmerman's book, *Shakedown: Exposing the Real Jesse Jackson,* there is no record that Jesse ever fulfilled the necessary requirements. He dropped out of the seminary and found someone to bestow the title Reverend on him. When I related the experience with both men to people, they were not surprised.

In January 2007, I discussed my Wal-Mart book with a magazine publisher. Wal-Mart not only advertises with this publisher, they have a good relationship. A few weeks later, I got over 40 emails and phone calls about a story Wal-Mart published in a major newspaper stating that Wal-Mart was looking for African companies to supply them with products. What an interesting coincidence?

In April 2007, a funding company sent me an email about a man who sold $45 million of product to Wal-Mart. I applaud his efforts. It takes a lot to do that much business with Wal-Mart. The email had a link to the man's audio tapes. After reading the email and listening to the audio tapes, several things he discussed regarding doing business with Wal-Mart bothered me. If his goal was to gain favor and do more business with Wal-Mart, it should work. I emailed the person who sent me the email. She forwarded my questions to him. He responded that Wal-Mart does not return products. Wal-Mart is notorious for returning products. He did not realize he was dialoguing with someone who did business with Wal-Mart. When I finally revealed who I was he stopped responding. The business experiences he shared definitely did not apply to minorities given that:

(a) he is not a minority owned company;

(b) his products are non-perishable (not food);

(c) he leveraged his friend's access to over 250 sales representatives and;

(d) even though he had very little money, someone financed his multi-million dollar deals.

GOOD SUPPLIER EXPERIENCE

You can tell the responsiveness of a company by looking at its management makeup. One day while watching television, a rarity for me, I watched an interview of Jim Sinegal, President of Costco. I was so impressed by how he spoke and the information revealed about Costco. The next day, I called his office leaving a message that I would like to sell Sheba Foods products to Costco. I was stunned to get a call back within 24 hours, from a member of his top management. The caller was a Black South African. I am told that Mr. Sinegal sometimes answers his phone.

Months later, I and other suppliers were invited to an all day event to present our products to the buyers. Many of Costco's top management were present throughout to answer any questions we had. Breakfast and lunch were provided. Detailed information was given. One-on-one meetings were setup with the appropriate buyer. I met with two buyers. Two current suppliers spoke about their Costco experience, both with glowing reports. The day ended with a tour of the Costco store, showing us potentially where our products could be placed. It helped in understanding Costco's need in terms of packaging and pricing. Anyone that wanted a complimentary day pass to shop at Costco that day got one. It was an awesome experience! Thereafter, whenever I called the buyers, my calls or emails were responded to immediately. I understand that experience was not unique to me. They are known for such responsiveness. Even if I never sell a single product to

Costco, I would not only shop there, but recommend others to do so. Months later, I saw two of the potential suppliers I met at the event and we still talked about the experience. We love Costco!

WAL-MART SUPPLIER DIVERSITY

Wal-Mart Supplier Diversity office is located in Bentonville, Arkansas. For the minority company wishing to do business with Wal-Mart in their region, a Local Supplier Questionnaire is required. The completed application is processed through the Wal-Mart Supplier Diversity office. My experience with Wal-Mart Supplier Diversity was good. The people cared. The Director at the time was a real asset in preventing havoc between me and Wal-Mart at an early stage.

Make no mistake, they pay attention to every microscopic detail of one's application making sure every Wal-Mart requirement is met prior to the products going to the buyer. When there were negative news to communicate, they did it professionally. A lot of companies now have Supplier Diversity departments which help minority companies navigate their products and/or services to the appropriate buyers. People expect more than they should out of companies' Supplier Diversity departments. They have no buying power or influence on one's product or service. Think of them as gatekeepers.

DOES THE WAL-MART SUPPLIER DIVERSITY PROGRAM WORK?

On the Wal-Mart website, it states "Wal-Mart is

committed to increasing and promoting the sourcing of merchandise and services from minority- and women-owned businesses."

Do they walk the talk?   Yes and No.

Yes.   The Wal-Mart Supplier Diversity program allows Wal-Mart to show the number of minority businesses that became new suppliers. Anyone would be impressed or at least back off if Wal-Mart showed a list of 50 or more companies that were given opportunities to sell products in their stores. If Wal-Mart were to show a list, to me it is a here today, gone tomorrow scenario. My Jollof Rice deli entry is one example. Here is another example. One day, I was in one of the Wal-Mart stores putting the products I delivered onto the freezer shelf. The District Manager and a Bentonville executive were inspecting the freezer products with the freezer manager. They picked up a new product that was in the freezer. I learned that it was recently delivered with no date on it. I heard "take that ..... off the shelf........" I did not see that product in the freezer thereafter. From then on, I made doubly sure that my products had dates on them. I felt that the company should have been given a warning and another chance. It is hard enough getting in and not fair to terminate the relationship abruptly. The product didn't get to test the market given the tremendous investment made in getting it approved.

No. I don't believe Wal-Mart walks the talk. Wal-Mart's new supplier's list would be justifiable if Wal-Mart shows the retention rate of the supplier. The questions that I asked Wal-Mart senior management, other Wal-Mart executives and Board Members were: "How many minority companies does Wal-Mart take on as new suppliers every year? How much business dollar wise is conducted with that supplier? How long is that supplier with Wal-Mart?" As of the time of the publishing of this book, Wal-Mart declined to answer. One of Wal-Mart's managers told me that the lifetime of most minorities suppliers in Wal-Mart is 90 days. He also stated that I should consider myself lucky that I lasted over two years. Since Wal-Mart declined to answer my questions and my Jollof Rice in the deli lasted 90 days, we will have to assume that the lifetime of a Wal-Mart minority supplier is 90 days.

BLESSINGS AND CURSES

I consider my product's entry into Wal-Mart both a blessing and a curse. A blessing because part of my target market shops at Wal-Mart and it got good exposure. A curse because most of life's basic enjoyment like sleep was replaced by much anxiety. I can't remember sleeping well in the two and a half years of the Wal-Mart relationship. Depression was a constant demon to deal with. Food became my drug of choice. I gained at least 40 pounds from December 2004 and August 2006 and 15 pounds in the three months of writing this book. Will they pull the product off the shelf tomorrow? Will the managers put the product where customers can't find it, and therefore it does not sell? Do I have the $150 per week per store for demo sales (marketing)? And so on, and so on. One of the things I had going for me was zero competition. There was no one else anywhere in the world that made my products; that has since changed. In 2007, there are at least two companies making similar products. Because there was no competition, there was no price pressure from Wal-Mart. They accepted the price I gave them. Most minority businesses are not in Wal-Mart long enough to experience prices pressures.

COMPETITION

More and more African products are making it into U.S. supermarkets. I get excited whenever I see an African product, one made in Africa, on a major U.S. supermarket shelf. I know the company is financially contributing to its community. Whoever gets into the major U.S. supermarket first, makes it much easier for others to follow. The first entrant breaks down the buyer's reservation on trying African products. All I have to do is make a better product with excellent packaging and have lower pricing. In practicing the saying, keep your friends close and your enemies closer, I choose to be close to my competition. It is always a pleasure speaking with my competition. I would call the company, get the owner on the line, introduce myself, let him or her know I've done my homework about their company and products, and see if there's room for collaboration. I met one of my competitors in 2005 at an event. She kept a distant and I knew there was no room for collaboration. At the time, she made pepper sauce. As of the writing of this book, she now has frozen Jollof Rice among other things.

The other competitor called me in 2006 and asked if I would represent her product. Does Coca-Cola sell Pepsi's products? No. I told her that my future plan for the frozen Sheba Stew is to make it shelf stable, in a can or bottle. Its current shelf stable state is the spice packets for both retail and food service. I expressed my concern for liability from her. She was willing to sign papers to remove this liability. Even though I like her spirit, I will never represent her product for obvious reasons. I do see future collaborations on African economic empowerment events.

SIGNATURES NEEDED ON WAL-MART'S LOCAL SUPPLIER QUESTIONNAIRE (LSQ)

I am glad that I started with a few stores prior to taking on 29 Wal-Mart stores. The first step in getting the products into the store is to get the LSQ signed. The signatures needed depend on these product categories:

(a) Food products: Food merchandiser (FM) & Store Manager.

(b) Non-food products: Store manager & District Manager.

Wal-Mart stores are grouped into districts. A minority supplier can apply to put their product in five districts at a time. The Wal-Mart FM generally has 14 stores located in more than one district. They can influence Store Managers in consideration of one's products. The Store Manager relies on the FM's evaluation and generally will not agree to a new product trial unless the FM approves of it. There was one FM I sensed right away would be a problem. Each time I called to set up a meeting to present my products, he stated he had a full schedule for weeks.

There is a Yoruba saying: "Ọ̀nọ kan kọ lo wọ ọja" English translation: "There's more than one way to get into the market." In exploring alternatives when faced with a major obstacle, I decided to get the Store and District Manager's signatures. Remember that for food products, only the FM and Store Manager's signatures are needed. I told the District Managers covering the stores I wanted, that given the uniqueness of my products, I needed them to not only be aware of my entry, but also needed their blessings. They gladly signed. I told the difficult FM's District Manager that the form was incomplete without the FM's signature. I requested the District Manager call the FM on my behalf.

I waited a week, called the FM, left a message, letting him know of the signatures I had. I continued that I would truly appreciate his signature to complete the application. He returned my call shortly thereafter, we met at six a.m. and he grudgingly signed the questionnaire. Of course, I thanked him profusely. He was not as compliant when it came time for his signature for the Jollof Rice's deli entry. The stores that I picked were in five districts covered by three FMs. The other two FMs were very supportive. I had no issues getting their signature both times—freezer and deli.

Prior to getting signatures for the LSQ, presentations were made to selected Wal-Mart management. A number of the meetings happened at six a.m. The meetings were early so the managers can attend to the daily running of their stores. From seven a.m., they attended to store meetings, deliveries, customer and employee issues. There were generally four or more people at any of my presentations — I, the Store Manager, District Manager, Freezer Manager or Deli Manager and FM. The presentations lasted about 30 minutes and went well. I came prepared with a marketing plan, left samples for them to try later (no one eats rice or stew at six a.m.). Depending on the location of the store, I had to leave home at three a.m. for the meetings. It was great preparation when it came time to deliver the products.

SIMPLIFYING WAL-MART LSQ REQUIREMENTS

The Supplier Diversity page on the Wal-Mart website gives details on requirements for product entry. In my opinion, the requirements help reduce the number of applicants. The application cost is a major factor. There is no fee to get the LSQ paper from the manager. The costs are in the documentation and certifications that must accompany the completed application.

One of Wal-Mart's requirements is that the suppliers have at least two years experience, a good thing. My prior supermarket exposure prepared me for the Wal-Mart experience. I am most grateful to the Ingles Supermarket's VP who helped define Sheba Foods' initial product line, and tried my products in a few stores. Ingles did not return a single product. At the end of the trial when it did not seem to be working, the VP said not to worry, they wrote it off. As a growing company, I really appreciated it. I had to reimburse Wal-Mart at the end of the product trial in the frozen section. There were no returns for the Jollof Rice in the Wal-Mart deli.

For all U.S. Supermarkets, getting the product into the store is one third of the battle, staying in is 2/3 of the battle. Of that 2/3s—one third is managing and servicing the product (delivery, marketing, product credit), the other 1/3 is managing the managers so they keep the product where it sells and hopefully order more.

The approximate cost for the documentation and certifications that need to accompany the Wal-Mart's LSQ is well over $4,500. Once application is approved there is no guarantee of getting the products on store shelves. The breakdown to be shown excludes travel expenses to Bentonville should the buyer require a face-to-face meeting, postage or new product packaging that may be required. The only time I could have gone to Bentonville, was when I was invited to meet with Wal-Mart senior management on issues with the deli Jollof Rice. Details in Chapter Five.

Using the LSQ for freezer and deli, I filled out the forms, made sure all requirements were met and sent all paperwork with empty packaging. Within three months, I got the news that the products and all the stores I wanted were approved. The first application got 29 stores and the second got 45 stores. Little did I know that the real struggle was about to begin. In my opinion, Wal-Mart does a great job of keeping minority companies out despite their mission statement.

Skip to Chapter 2 if not curious about the Wal-Mart requirements or not thinking of selling to Wal-Mart. The next few pages breaks down the requirements and potential $4,500+ investment needed to complete the LSQ.

REQUIRED BUSINESS CERTIFICATIONS — COST $500 TO $6,000

One of these business certifications is required — Women's Business Enterprise (WBE) or Minority Business Enterprise certification (MBE). Sheba Foods is a certified WBE and was a certified MBE till December 31st, 2006. Both certifications help companies get audience with major corporations and can result in contracts. Current fees are listed on both organizations' website and it can take up to six months to be certified. Sheba Foods' cost was $500 to $600 for each because I processed the application myself. It could have been up to $6,000 if I had used a consultant. One of the services Sheba Foods offers is consultancy, assisting companies with their business certifications. There are many hoops to jump through prior to being certified. Financial statements, board and shareholders meetings notes and other documentation must be submitted with application. Site visit of company is part of the application process. I decided to not renew my MBE membership for it seemed redundant to have both certifications. I have not gotten any new business from having either. Both certifications were good networking tools with fellow WBE and MBE companies.

WBE website: http://www.wbenc.org

MBE website: http://www.nmsdcus.org

DUN & BRADSTREET NUMBER—COST $75

Dun and Bradstreet (D & B) is a provider of credit reports on international and U.S. businesses. D & B assigns a unique number to each company which allows others to report positive or negative information. The information once analyzed, rates the company's credit worthiness, and can translate to the Wal-Mart Supplier Evaluation Report. The report must have a rating less than 7 to meet Wal-Mart's requirements. The D & B report is a show stopper. A supplier could have all the requirements, if the report is 7 or higher, no further processing of one's application can be done. I highly recommend this be the supplier's first step. It makes sense to proceed with the remaining requirements once there is clearance with the D & B report.

D & B has an office exclusively for Wal-Mart suppliers. Their phone number is (866) 815-2749. If the supplier does not have a D & B number, call the dedicated office. They will take all necessary information over the phone and forward it to the main D & B office. Within three to five days a representative from the main D & B office will contact the supplier to complete the application. Shortly thereafter, a D & B number is assigned and Supplier Evaluation Report generated. As of August 2007, the cost for the Supplier Evaluation Report is $75, for new or existing suppliers.

Per my experience, Wal-Mart can require a D & B Supplier Evaluation Report at any time. A good time to request it is when the supplier to be eliminated desires to add a new product. D & B's erroneous report surprised me for many businesses base their business decisions on those reports. Chapter Four shares how D & B's reporting gave Wal-Mart a justifiable business reason to prevent my Jollof Rice entry into the deli.

INSURANCE REQUIREMENTS - COST $3,200+

Please visit the Wal-Mart website for exact insurance coverage needed, then contact your commercial insurance agent for pricing. Insurance premiums vary per product.

(1) Liability insurance — can be $2,500+ for $2 million coverage. Other food products may require more than $2 million coverage.

(2) Worker's Compensation — can start at $1,200. Using a cost of $400 per employee per year, with three employees = $400 x 3. This covers the supplier's employees who deliver products in the Wal-Mart stores.

(3) Employers' Liability insurance — prices vary. This insurance is needed should any of the supplier's employee become injured.

UCC MEMBERSHIP NUMBER - COST $750

I think of the Universal Code Council (UCC) number as a way to track a product back to the manufacturer. It also serves as an inventory tool. A copy of the membership letter showing the five digit code must accompany the completed LSQ. A UPC label, another Wal-Mart requirement, can then be generated once the UCC number is issued. The cost for a new UCC registration is $750. Call UCC at (937) 435-3870 for current fees and questions. One option in significantly reducing this cost is to partner with someone who already has a registration.

A sample of a UPC label - includes the UCC number.

1. The first and last digits are generated by the computer program that creates the barcode. In this example it is 0 (Zero) and 6 (Six).

2. The next five digit (83006) are the numbers UCC assigns.

3. The last five digits (12002) are made up by supplier.

I hope that the Wal-Mart requirements have been simplified for the potential supplier or the curious reader. It is the unstated rules and practices that keep one from getting into Wal-Mart regardless of fulfillment of their requirements. Once the application is completed and the product approved, a supplier number is issued. If the buyer had not approved my products, a letter about the decision would have been sent.

MISCELLANEOUS EXPENSES TO PONDER

The $4,500 is the initial investment. There are additional expenses that I incurred once my products were approved. I share them here as a reminder that there are additional investments to be made.

Marketing Expenses

1. *Demo expenses.* A demo is when small amounts of a product are given to potential customers to taste, hoping they'll buy. My supermarket experience showed that demos are the most effective marketing tool in selling products. Demos are one of the unstated but expected supplier service once the product is on the store shelf. To aid the approval of my products, I included a letter to the buyer detailing a marketing plan. Wal-Mart referred me to their four approved demo sales companies. The average cost of a demo is $150 per store per week. I had to convince the buyer to allow me to do my demos, giving me control over the cost.

   My argument to the buyer was simple. Presentation is everything. Most of the time, the approved companies' staff are elderly (retired) and not passionate about the products they are marketing. I could not see how they would effectively sell African foods. Their staff uniform is a white top and black bottom. The Sheba Foods' presentation is African—

table setup and uniform.   A presentation that drew customers to our table.

2. *Postcards* — gave these out during demos and every where I went.

3. *Website* — an invaluable tool in showcasing one's products. Please visit us at www.shebafoods.com.

4. *Sponsorships* — cash investment in events or product donations.

Order taking & Transportation Expenses

5. *Sales Representatives* - I didn't use any, but should have. I am told they work solely on commission — 3% to 5%. We are currently looking for sales representatives. Please contact us if able to gets us new markets.

6. **Transportation costs** - I opted to deliver my products by Direct Store Delivery (DSD) to all 29 stores. A time consuming and exhaustive task. However, it was one of the best decisions I made, because I learned a lot.

    (a) Got to negotiate better spacing for my product.

    (b) Learned how shelf price labels were generated.

    (c) Watched how the other delivery people conducted business and dealt with the Wal-Mart receivers.

Chapter Two

Wal-Mart's Partial Track Record

Behind every great fortune
is a great crime!
Honoré de Balzac

       This Chapter gives an overview of Wal-Mart from a shopper and supplier perspective. I've tried to keep the discussion of facts simple. Sources are listed in the various Chapters, as well as, in Reference at the back of the book. As a shopper, I didn't care how the products got there. It was a good price and I bought it. My supplier experience broaden my knowledge. I still shopped at Wal-Mart after they kicked my products out. Doing research for this book revealed information that reduced my shopping at Wal-Mart. Realistically, how many people take the time to research Wal-Mart? Most definitely not the shoppers.

POSITIVES

I was not aware of all these Wal-Mart positives prior to putting my products at Wal-Mart. Looking back, these positives justified my being a Wal-Mart supplier. I would assume these positives are shared by thousands of companies who have their products in Wal-Mart and others who try to put their products in Wal-Mart.

1. *Seduced by the thousands of stores.* As of July 15, 2007, Wal-Mart had 6,981 stores - 4,068 in the U.S. and 2,913 International locations. Those numbers of stores wheel a lot of buying and influential power. I was definitely one of those seduced by almost 7,000 Wal-Mart's stores.

2. *High sales.* The Jollof Rice deli entry into only 45 stores presented a sales opportunity of over $1 million. Imagine the product placed in 1,000 stores.

3. *Improved business efficiency.* Wal-Mart is known for continuous improvement in its ability to handle, move, and track merchandise. This strength translated into Sheba Foods' business operations, which became more structured, efficient and focused during the Wal-Mart experience.

4. *Credibility.* I was told by companies that being a Wal-Mart supplier gave Sheba Foods' financial credibility. It takes a lot to get Wal-Mart's approval. Suppliers that pass Wal-Mart's due diligence are perceived financially sound and stable.

5. *High employment.* An increase in staff becomes a benefit with the new Wal-Mart business. I had to hire more staff once I became a supplier.

NEGATIVES

I at no point in time considered any of these negatives in my quest to become a Wal-Mart supplier. I believe that naiveness kept me alive in Wal-Mart.

1. *Bankruptcy.* Using the previous example, now imagine what happens if the product is pulled out overnight in all 1,000 stores. Devastating! If I had assumed the number of stores would grow and in that anticipation, went ahead and made major capital investment solely for servicing Wal-Mart, this pull-out would lead to bankruptcy. One of the reasons Wal-Mart mandates that they be only 20% of the supplier's business is so that when the Wal-Mart business ceases, the supplier's 80% can sustain its financial survival.

2. *Squeeze on low price.* Wal-Mart's goal is to buy product from suppliers cheaper every year, so Wal-Mart can sell it cheaper.

3. *Open financials.* I have heard of instances where Wal-Mart demanded and examined suppliers' private financial records to justify their reason to do business.

4. *Dictation of company's direction.* Given Wal-Mart's buying power and knowing that the supplier wants to remain a supplier, Wal-Mart makes concessions that may cause a loss for the supplier.

5. *Uncertainty of product's stay.* Here today, gone tomorrow scenario. A product can be pulled off the shelf at any time for no reason.

Yes, Wal-Mart's negative track record was everywhere for those who are looking for it. I was not one of them. As a matter of fact I did not want to know. I focused on the positives. My mind frame at the time is best explained with this story:

> Two frogs fell into a well. One of them was deaf. The other frog was of good hearing and spoke. The deaf frog kept jumping up against the wall, attempting to climb out of the well. The good hearing frog kept telling the deaf frog to give it up, that it is useless and a waste of time to keep trying to get out of the well. Let them just accept their fate that death is eminent. The deaf frog of course saw the talking frog's lips moving and gesturing but didn't understand what was said. The talking frog got tired of talking and went to sleep. The deaf frog kept trying and succeeded in climbing out of the well. Did he go back and help the other frog get out? You decide!

I didn't tell a soul I was applying to Wal-Mart, not even my husband. My research on Wal-Mart was as simple as: I shop there most of the time. They should sell my product for they didn't have any African products in any of their stores. It was hard to not be aware of Wal-Mart's negative track record. People offered me condolences instead of congratulations when I told them my products were in Wal-Mart. It was discouraging, but I shrouded it off.

I came across a fascination, gusty story about an executive, Jim Wier whose former company is headquartered in Georgia. The complete story is in Chapter

Five of Charles Fishman's book *The Wal-Mart Effect*, titled: *The Man Who Said No to Wal-Mart*. How courageous Jim Wier was in telling Wal-Mart he would no longer sell to them. He should be in the Guinness book of World Records. Given Sheba Foods is also located in Georgia, I thought I would look up Mr. Wier, have lunch and conversation with him. He is my kind of person, someone for me to learn from. In June 2007, I called his company and was told he retired in 2005. No longer affiliated with the company. The executive I spoke with gave no contact information to reach him. When asked, he added the company's lawn movers have not returned to Wal-Mart. This was not the only company that refused to do business with Wal-Mart. The other company's story is at the end of this Chapter.

I relate to Mr. Wier's story in many ways—his experience, logic in regards to his products, the direction and health of his company. Jim Wier's strategy in regards to the perception of his products, was quality over price. He was not seduced at all by the millions of dollars his company would be losing from the decision he made. He was firm on not selling to Wal-Mart. I read that not selling to Wal-Mart, helped maintain his lawn movers high quality image, and loyalty of independent distributors. I would love to know if his sales increased through his independent distributors, making up for the Wal-Mart lost sales. I would guess that many people respected his unprecedented decision, and bought his lawn movers because of his decision not to sell to Wal-Mart. I would have been one of them.

When you think of Wal-Mart, do you think quality? No, you think made in China. You think cheap. Be honest. Sheba Foods' brand and the other company products that we represent are all natural, no preservative products. Many people tell me that in order to maintain my products' gourmet image, my products should not be in Wal-Mart.

In May 2007, I bought bicycles in Wal-Mart for my daughters. They broke within two weeks. The department manager offered to repair them instead of taking back, even though I presented a receipt. No sooner we got the bicycle back from repair, the pedals broke. In early June 2007, we returned one of the bikes for a new one. The same day we brought the new bike home, the pedal broke—my daughter yelled "not again!" and busted into tears. I told her it was not her fault and that we'll get her a better bike. Face it Wal-Mart has low prices and the quality is not always there. How can the quality be there given suppliers have to make and sell their products cheaper each year? You get what you pay for.

Who is Wal-Mart's target market? Statistics show the average income of Wal-Mart shoppers is $35,000 and generally of low education. Wal-Mart's competitions attract higher income and education shoppers. Another interesting fact is that 57% of Southerners in the U.S. shop at Wal-Mart regularly, compared to only 24% of U.S. Northeasterners. The Northeast is considered more affluent (higher income), fast paced, more educated and cultured, while the Southeast is the opposite. Is this to say that the education level is so low, that price is the only concern of the Southeastern shoppers? If yes, then my products definitely should not retail in Wal-Mart.

MAJOR ISSUES FOR THE AFRICAN SUPPLIER TO CONSIDER

I need to take a moment and speak to my African brothers and sisters wanting to sell their products in the U.S., especially to Wal-Mart. The points below may also apply to foreign, non-African suppliers. In marketing non-competing African brands, I discovered that many African companies have an illusion about selling their products in the U.S. The risk is much greater doing business with companies that have 100% return guarantee. Should this option be exercised, the African company will incur major losses. These are the four major issues:

Payment: This is the frequently asked question by the African suppliers who want me to represent their products. We only do consignment. Payment can be three to four months after the order is shipped from their country. Let say the order ships today. It takes a month for the ocean freight to reach the U.S. About two weeks to clear customs if there are no product issues at the port. It is now six weeks. Let say it takes another two weeks to deliver the product to the stores. Now at eight weeks and the payment clock starts. Most supermarkets have a 30-45 day payment timeline. Once the supermarket check clears, it can take five days to remit payment to the supplier. That is almost four months from the day the order shipped.

Returns: The U.S. supplier has numerous issues selling to Wal-Mart, and they are in the same country. The African supplier can successfully sell to Wal-Mart as long as it is in bulk, with a zero percent return policy. In the African marketplace, there is no such thing as a return. Once I buy the product, I might be able to exchange it, otherwise, I own it forever. Product placement in U.S.

supermarkets present major losses when pulled off the shelves for lack of sales. All monies previously paid to the supplier for the returned products must be refunded immediately to the supermarkets. When my Wal-Mart freezer trial ended, I had to refund Wal-Mart for the products they claimed were left. The other losses for the African supplier are freight costs, demo expenses and other marketing investment. When I tell the African supplier to prepare for this business practice, they look at me strangely.

Marketing: The African supplier thinks that once the product is on the shelf it is a done deal. Not so, someone needs to market it so it sells, for the buyer to order more. Wal-Mart will not and does not contribute a single cent to the supplier's marketing. I don't know of any supermarket that contributes to marketing. It is entirely up to the supplier to market (sell) the products in the store. A few stores may give the supplier prime space at no cost. A space which big companies pay what is called slotting fees for (more on this in Chapter Six). That prime space puts the product at high visibility and can result in great sales.

Strategy: One must have an entry and exit strategy going into any company. One of my entry strategies is getting as much exposure as possible—lots of demos, stories in the media, event sponsorship, internet marketing and monthly e-newsletters. Sheba Foods sends out newsletters with African recipes, product information, nutritional facts and other news we feel is beneficial to our subscribers. Please visit our website www.shebafoods.com and subscribe to receive our newsletter.

That completes the major issues for the African supplier.

WAL-MART'S LOW PRICES

Wal-Mart's goal is to sell all products cheaper every year. Most companies' strategies, Sheba Foods included, is to produce better products every year, hopefully without increasing price. To do that requires better raw materials, capital investment in equipment or computer systems, recruitment and/or training of staff — all of which would increase overhead. The investments in having a better product can result in increased price. So how do you stay in Wal-Mart maintaining high quality, while Wal-Mart sells it cheaper year after year? Not always possible.

An alternative is to produce two versions of the same product. I know that a number of companies produce high and low end products which Wal-Mart suggested to Jim Wier. The ethical Jim Wier refused. He was not going to allow Wal-Mart to dictate his product line. The companies with both versions of product, put the high quality products in one chain store and the low end products in another chain store. As a consumer, this is an issue for me. How do I know that the low quality product is not tagged with a high quality label and price? I most likely would not buy from this company. What does that say about the company's ethics? If other companies did as Jim, Wal-Mart would be filled with inferior products at low prices or high end products at premium prices. How many people do you think would then shop at Wal-Mart?

WHAT'S THE COMPLAINT ABOUT WAL-MART?

The complaints are many and appropriately documented on the internet. I spent a whole week reading about the complaints, court cases and other practices. I was overwhelmed by the information. There are numerous organizations that actively campaign against Wal-Mart. To find them Google anti-Wal-Mart groups.

The wakeupwalmart.com website has many pages of facts, they could write a book. The website offered information and assistance to Wal-Mart workers to come together, learn about their workplace rights, and build a new empowering movement, hoping to change Wal-Mart into a responsible employer. Many of the complaints were confirmed in Robert Greenwald's movie. One would think that with so many adversaries, Wal-Mart would have made more positive changes to its business practices.

Many of these Wal-Mart complaints surprised me:

1. *Disrupting communities they enter.* Bankrupting small businesses in the area Wal-Mart enters, which goes against the American dream.

2. *No health insurance for many of its employees.* Those that have Wal-Mart's health insurance claim that it is not sufficient to meet their family's needs. Wal-Mart's health coverage is far below its competitor's offerings.

3. *Little or no retirement benefit* for its employees.

4. *Pays very low wages* compared to it competitors. There are Wal-Mart employees that receive welfare, meaning that they are on government subsidy. The Wal-Mart employees' pay is so low, they receive food stamps to buy food and on government healthcare.

This was one of the facts that I spent time studying because I couldn't see how it could be true, but it is.

Wal-Mart benefits four ways (a) it makes money from selling product to its shoppers; (b) the employees' paycheck goes back to Wal-Mart for they shop there for their families (c) if the shopper is a tax payer, their taxes is used to subsidize the Wal-Mart employee's family whose wages puts them on welfare; (d) whether or not I shop at Wal-Mart, my taxes go to subsidize those same Wal-Mart employees. What a sweet deal!

5. *Practices the same long hours with no pay*, and child labor violations found in many underdeveloped countries.

6. *Spends more money on advertising*, donations to politicians and other expenditures than its employees' healthcare and development.

In 2005, during my deli ordeal, I had the pleasure of communicating with Brad Seligman. He is the attorney handling the lawsuit charging Wal-Mart with discrimination against its female workers—*Dukes v. Wal-Mart Stores' case.* I applaud Mr. Seligman for taking on this enormous case. The number of plaintiffs could be up to 1.6 million women. The gender discrimination lawsuit, alleges that female employees were discriminated against in pay and promotions. In February 2007, the United States Court of Appeals for the Ninth Circuit issued a 2-1 ruling that affirmed a lower court ruling in favor of the plaintiffs. According to *USA Today*, there were 5,000 lawsuits in the year 2000 against Wal-Mart, more lawsuits than any other company in the United States. The *Dukes v. Wal-Mart Stores* lawsuit is one that I hope Wal-Mart loses. It would be significant in changing Wal-Mart's ethical direction.

How can a company with such high sales mistreat its suppliers and employees? Wal-Mart's billions of dollars in profit would be significantly reduced, if they paid their employees fairly, and not squeeze prices to such low points with their suppliers. Wal-Mart can afford to pay its workers well. It just doesn't. It can treat its suppliers as well as its competition, it chooses not to. With all the negatives, many companies still want to be suppliers and many more people shop there. I can't blame people for trying to survive and provide for their families. This is why I feel the pressure for Wal-Mart to be responsible needs to come from those in position of power. For example, instead of the government subsidizing Wal-Mart operations, it should require that Wal-Mart pay appropriate wages and provide sufficient health care for its employees.

CHANGE IS POSSIBLE FOR WAL-MART

In my opinion, it is almost impossible to win a lawsuit against Wal-Mart. They have too much money, too many people (politicians, etc.) on their payroll. Their legal team is skilled in prolonging and/or camouflaging any issue. Prior to Attorney Seligman's lawsuit, Wal-Mart ranked well below its retailing peers in the placement of female employees and their placement in management roles. In 2001, the numbers of females in Wal-Mart's management was 30%. Shortly thereafter came the female discrimination case. On April 3, 2007, per Wikipedia, Wal-Mart reported that female employees were now 61% of its workforce and 40% of its management. I think this was Wal-Mart's attempt to show compliant and prove that the lawsuit should be dismissed.

In November 2005, Robert Greenwald released his movie, *Wal-Mart, the High Cost of Low Price*. It did an excellent job in waking up the American consciousness about who is suffering to make possible Wal-Mart's low prices. Robert Greenwald's movie forced Wal-Mart to make many positive changes. I hope this book gets Wal-Mart to make positive changes in its suppliers' relations.

I knew my Wal-Mart frustration was not unique and sought out other businesses with similar experiences. In July 2006, I sent an email to my subscribers. Asked for stories from companies who were doing business, had done business or had interactions with Wal-Mart. The responses were confirmation that I should write this book and share my experience with the World. Who knows, others may be encouraged to do the same. Don't sue, write a book! Trust me it is cheaper and great therapy.

Within 48 hours of sending the newsletter, I got a call from the Wal-Mart VP who oversees the entire food buying for Wal-Mart. More on him in Chapter Five. He said: "Ms. Oluleye, I became aware that you had sent out a newsletter that reflects negatively on Wal-Mart. Do you know how that came to be?" I responded: "Hello, Mr. _ _." Trying not to chuckle. "Yes, I sent it and can tell you exactly how you got it." It came from Y because Y was on the distribution list." The VP did not deny Y sent him the newsletter. He was quite surprised that I had the audacity to tell him who gave him the information and not afraid of Wal-Mart's reaction.

What was Wal-Mart going to do? Kick my product out of the stores? At that time, they had already done their worst. I felt that it was my turn to be in control. The VP went on to tell me that the newsletter was not appreciated.

I responded that I didn't appreciate how my products had been treated. The conversation ended politely. Till today, I've kept three Wal-Mart management on my distribution list. Why? Strategy and Therapy. I want Wal-Mart updated on my progress.

Below are two of the stories from companies that responded to my newsletter request. Company information has been removed or changed to protect their identities. However, the Wal-Mart personnel reading this knows who they are because I mentioned both situations to Wal-Mart.

Dear Sheba Foods:

I have received your newsletter in the past and was thrilled to see that at least some minorities were successful in getting into Wal-Mart. I am equally disappointed to learn of your problems. I am the owner and creator of ABC company here in Blank city. For months I was in contact with the Wal-Mart Supplier Diversity.

I contacted both of them and spoke in detail about the local program and how to get in. I met with several local Wal-Mart managers and district managers and they were ALL very excited and approved of having my cards in their stores. I got all the paperwork filled out with the necessary signatures, UPC code, etc. and jumped through all the other hoops. I did everything else requested as part of the local program and although I was in constant contact with the buyer, my products were not approved.

Needless to say, I was very disappointed. The buyer never gave me specific reasons as to why my product were not approved. I got nothing but praise regarding my packaging, pricing, etc. I think the real reason why they turned me down was because of an explicit or implicit exclusivity agreement they may have with the Hallmark company.

The buyer never said this was the reason but I have noticed there are no other greeting card companies in Wal-Mart stores. Indeed it was very frustrating to go through the whole process only to be turned down at the very end.

So, I certainly did not have a good experience with trying to get into Wal-Mart. As I said earlier, all the Wal-Mart managers I contacted were thrilled with the prospect of my cards coming into their stores, but the buyer for whatever reason, did not approve them. I hope this information is beneficial to you. I want to keep trying and would appreciate any suggestions you can share.

My response to this writer was that it would be nice if Wal-Mart would communicate its exclusivity agreements to minority suppliers, so as to not waste their time and limited resources. This supplier would have spent the time and resources on other alternatives.

Dear Sheba Foods:

This past October (that would be 2005), Wal-Mart asked my company for a bid to do an audit of their telephone invoices. It came down to us and another company. We had two meetings at their offices in Bentonville and I told them in our first meeting that we would not work for free for them, that we had single moms that counted on us. We bid the work at 30%, our lowest price and our competitor that won the business bid 3%. Wal-Mart told us that they had chosen them to do the work. Wal-Mart was to give them a report card. Wal-Mart wouldn't have to pay them a penny if the report card fails to get a "B" or above. I couldn't believe what I was being told. First, there is no way the company can make money at 3%, we were at our bottom price at 30%. I think that they should be ashamed of themselves.

Also, I sat beside the Wal-Mart Supplier Diversity group at the WBENC conference in Miami two weeks ago and told them the story and they couldn't believe it themselves. So, I honestly have to say that I and my staff thank God that we did not sign Wal-Mart. We don't shop at Wal-Mart and haven't for the past 4 years and have canceled our Sam's cards.

Imagine that! Is the company Wal-Mart chose destined for bankruptcy? As I read this letter, two thoughts came to mind. *One:* the company who won the bid wanted in at all costs. *Two:* the company may be using this Wal-Mart entry to get into other Wal-Mart areas where they can be profitable or get other non-Wal-Mart business.

Chapter Three

Sheba Foods' Freezer Experience

Faith is taking the first step even
when you don't see the whole staircase.
Martin Luther King

Many of the names, letters, emails, documents between me, Wal-Mart and others were left out of this book for many reasons. The fear of a lawsuit was not one of them. In the event that those talked about have a temper tantrum, then the concealed information will be revealed.

In 2007, Sheba Foods turned 4-years old! Whew!!! Many lessons learned. Many failures and successes. In 2003, Sheba Foods' products debuted in a major regional supermarket called Ingles, giving me the first major supermarket exposure. A great preparation for Wal-Mart.

Getting into Wal-Mart was the second easiest thing that I've done. Ingles was the first easiest. I have three children all born through Caesarean sections. The nine months of pregnancy was hell on earth, resulting in three angels God gave me a privilege to care for. I've never met any of the Wal-Mart buyers that approved my products. I'll never been to Bentonville. My application got approved through the mail, within three months and I managed to stay alive in Wal-Mart for almost two and a half years. When I compare the pregnancies and childbirth to supermarket entries, the supermarket entries were much easier. Glory be to God!

When I started four years ago, I had very little knowledge about the commercial food industry. People laughed when I told them that Sheba Foods was founded out of the desperation to survive. Necessity truly was the mother of invention. My husband had lost his job and I needed to help support the family. I love sharing my experiences because I have found that many people benefit from it. I try as much as I can to be real, not embarrassed to allow people to see me at my weak points. That's life. Who knows, by my sharing, they may have a solution for me.

I shared experiences in getting my products into stores in my book: *Selling My Food to Supermarkets, Distributors, Etc.* The book details encounters with buyers, some good, others not so good. It gives guidance to suppliers who want to take their product to any market, not limited to the food industry. It also tells the story as to how this African woman crossed various barriers: cultural, race, gender, faith and issues of being a small business.

Common sense told me I needed a mentor. I called numerous people that I thought could fulfill that role. All were impressed about my entry into Wal-Mart, but declined either feeling they were not qualified to mentor me or too busy. A few asked if I would be their mentor given the numerous challenges that I had overcome. I am still looking for a mentor—no preference of gender or industry. It would be great if the person is a woman. My mentor has to be someone who has failed miserably, dusted it off to rise to higher greatness. There is so much to learn from failure. It is then one discovers what one is made of. I heard that success is how high one bounces when one hits the bottom.

An entrepreneur is creative. I had to be creative given I had very little money when Sheba Foods was birth. Having an MBA helped in understanding and structuring Sheba Foods. I did "creative" financing, taking all my jewelry to the pawn shop. I got them out many months later. I tried to factor my Wal-Mart invoices to generate the additional funds needed. No funding company would factor the Wal-Mart invoices because of the 100% product return policy. Factoring is a funding method where finance companies buy invoices, similar to banks buying debt, charging the client a percentage of the amount. Factoring is not a long-term solution and is expensive even in the short-term. I was blessed that my suppliers accepted payment once Wal-Mart paid me. The "creative" financing worked well.

Once in Wal-Mart, Sheba Foods growing pains became intense. There are days that I did not sleep for 72 hours, feeding the anxiety with overeating. A year or so into the Wal-Mart relationship, I felt like quitting. In sharing my frustration with a friend, I got the Nelson Mandela's poem shown on the back of the acknowledgement page. At first, I read it as it was written. It then became "Kunmi, your deepest fear is not that you are inadequate, it seems so at times. Just look at what you've accomplished. Kunmi, your deepest fear is that you are powerful beyond measure. You've gone and continue to go where angels fear to thread. It is your light, not your darkness, that frightens you and others most. You sometimes ask yourself, who are you to be brilliant, gorgeous, talented and fabulous? The better question is, who are you not to be?" Tears started rolling down my face.

I went back to the beginning of the poem. In reading it again, many of the "You" became "I". I hand wrote the entire poem substituting "I, my" for "You, our" as it came to my spirit. I read it out loud many times the new way, crying for hours thereafter. What possessed me to get into Wal-Mart? The stress for the past months came out through those flood of tears. It is true that I am brilliant, gorgeous, talented, fabulous and being a child of God is what has gotten me this far. Why quit now? Getting into Wal-Mart proved that I am meant to shine. God says that he'll never give me more than I can handle, so I deserve to be a supplier. How many minority companies like me has gotten in?

New "Friends" once in Wal-Mart

Getting my products into Wal-Mart definitely increased my number of "friends." I call them fair weathered friends. A network which the net did not work. Like any success, there were those who identified with success and cared nothing about me. They wanted to see what was in it for them. Can I get their products into Wal-Mart? Can I sponsor their events? Can I advertise in their magazine or on their website?   They thought I was rich since I sold to Wal-Mart. As time passed, because I did not put out as much as they expected, they were gone! It is going to be interesting seeing how many new "friends" I lose or gain once this book is published.

THE WAL-MART JOURNEY BEGAN

In December 2003, I filled out the freezer paperwork for four products — Jollof Rice, Sheba Stew, Melon Gourmet (Egusi) and Jute Soup (called Ewedu in Yoruba). I got the signed LSQ, letter to the buyer, product packaging, and sent it to Wal-Mart Supplier Diversity. In less than three months, on March 2, 2004, I got the news that all the products and stores that I submitted to the buyer were approved! I can add new products and new districts every six months. I was so excited! Jumped up and down for at least 15 minutes, screaming Halleluyah all over the house. Thank God I was the only one home that day. My kids would have concluded that their Mother had lost her mind.

After I calmed down, I called to thank the buyer and asked for next steps. I soon found out my excitement would be short lived. I was told to take the buyer's letter to petition each of the Store's frozen food managers for their order. Together, we determined where to place the product. The Wal-Mart approval letter gives no guarantee of an order or sales to Wal-Mart. All products that are approved through the Local Supplier Questionnaire (LSQ) are not built into the store's planogram (*see glossary*). The buyer leaves it entirely up to the managers to decide if they want the product in the store. Why go through all the trouble of getting approved, if there is no hope of putting the product in any store?

To me this is a brilliant Wal-Mart scheme to show the number of approved minority suppliers. The approval letter gave me audience with the managers, that's all. It does not mean they'll do one cent of business with me. At least, we gave them the opportunity which by the way came with a $4,500+ price. This Wal-Mart buyer arrangement allows the managers to give me legitimate business reasons for not having space in the freezer. The word "category management" came up in various conversations with the managers. It simply means that for them to put a new product on the shelf, an existing product must be taken off. That happened in a few stores.

Let's recap, I got the LSQ signed by the managers to get started. Now that Bentonville has approved the products, I have to go back to the managers to see if they are still interested, and have space on their shelves for my products. Also keep in mind that by the time the questionnaire is approved, given the high turnover at Wal-Mart, the manager could have moved to another department, quit or fired. Just when I thought all was clear, it presented another hurdle to overcome.

SHEBA FOODS' WAL-MART PRODUCT AGREEMENT

1. Payment for products delivery was set to 30 days.

2. My delivery method was Direct Store Delivery (DSD) which included:

    (a) Getting the products to the store.

(b) Putting it on the shelf, in this case the freezer.

3. Returns & Credit

(a) Pick up damaged units.

(b) Exchange or issue credit for damaged items.

ABOUT THE PRODUCTS

These are the products approved for 29 stores located in five districts.

Jollof Rice originated from Senegal & Gambia. This West African favorite dish combines rice and tangy spices. In Senegal, it is commonly prepared by the Wolof people, who add various meats and vegetables. Gambians make a similar dish with rice and fish dish. They call it Ceebu Jën. Jollof rice became popular as people traded goods back and forth in West Africa. Jollof Rice is the Mother of Jambalaya. When it came to the U.S. it became Jambalaya. As it traveled to the Caribbean, it became Seasoned Rice. When it got to Latin America it became Paella.

16 ounce Jollof Rice   16 ounce Sheba Stew

Sheba Stew is a medley of tomatoes, onions, pepper, garlic, other spices and olive oil. It can be spicy. Originated in Nigeria, known as Obe in the Yoruba culture. Also served in other West African countries. This delicious stew gives you a base to create a unique taste for you and your guests. The Sheba Foods website has recipes on how to Create-A-Stew with Meat, Chicken, Fish, Shrimp or Tofu. This stew has endless possibilities.

Please visit our website to view the Melon Gourmet and Jute Soup.

Melon Gourmet is a West African favorite fondly known as Egusi. An exceptionally rich vegetable medley with spinach, melon seeds, tomatoes, onions and spices. Best served with Africa's favorite starches, Fufu, Pounded Yam, Roasted Cassava (Gari) or Rice. Excellent with Sheba Stew.

Jute Soup originated among Egyptians during the time of the Pharaohs. It is a traditional dish in Egypt and Sudan, and a West African favorite. Jute soup is a variation of the Egyptian Molokhia (Molokeyhia), a moist & sticky, nutritious soup. This was one of the products that stunned the people who generated the Nutrition Facts. They could not believe the results and I was equally impressed. My Mother fed us this delicious dark green soup religiously when I was a child. It is truly one of Africa's hidden secrets.

Jute Soup has 210% Vitamin A & 110% Vitamin C.

MANAGER MEETINGS & THEIR NIGERIAN PHOBIAS

I met with 29 frozen food managers within a 150-mile radius. It took over six weeks for the meetings giving their schedules. Many of them were not in the initial presentations, the meetings that were held at six a.m. These managers had not been told by their District Managers and Food Merchandisers about the possibility of African foods for their freezers. They questioned the validity of my approved paperwork. I gave them photocopies of the buyer's approval letter for verification with Bentonville, but most importantly place their order.

I remember a number of the managers asked of my nationality. I proudly said Nigeria, not sharing that I am a U.S. citizen. They were now sure the paperwork was not valid. I chuckled. A few of the managers shared that they got the "419" fraudulent emails. They wanted to be sure that I stated Nigeria as my country of origin. I smiled, repeated proudly Nigeria, and shared that I too got the emails and simply delete them. It takes two to tango. The sender plays on the receiver's greed. If I don't respond, the sender has nothing to get from me. I recommended the managers block the emails or delete them. The managers looked on curiously. I refused to get upset or give them an excuse to not try the products.

The next section share the thoughts that went through my mind, which I restrained myself from sharing. I stated in *About the Book* that it was hard keeping emotions out of this book. This is one of the instances.

You may want to skip to the next italics heading, page 61, because this section is the education I would have given those Wal-Mart managers. There were many things that I wanted to tell those Wal-Mart managers. Two were that I did not chose to be black, nor did I chose to be Nigerian. I definitely was not apologizing for other people's actions. It was not the time to educate them that Nigerians have made, and still making major positive contributions to every fabric of American and World's economy. We are trailblazers. I am the first African (Nigerian) to put Ready-to-eat Authentic African Cuisine in major U.S. supermarkets. A Yoruba man who migrated to Ireland seven years ago became Mayor in Ireland, June 2007. Compliments to the Irish people for open mindedness and embracing diversity. Watch the Irish economy boom for their diversity effort. Nigerians are among the top highly educated people in the World. Look at multi-global financial establishments, top medical and educational institutions. There is a Nigerian in top management, if not the top management. There are numerous homes in many parts of Nigeria, especially in Abuja, the capital city, which would make multi-million dollar houses in the United States look like servant quarters. A friend of mine, Dr. Ugorji has a book and television show in the U.S. called *Tall Drums*, which profiles numerous Nigerian contributions to the American fabric. Let's not forget that the impact of Nigeria's oil on the U.S.

Sometimes, I think common sense is not so common. Do we not teach our children to not talk to strangers? Yet, a stranger sends me an email offering me a percentage of millions and I trust the person. Does the person not have a brother, sister or relative they could make the same offer? Another "419" email is lottery winnings. I must play the lottery in other to win! Why would anyone believe they won the lottery when they did not play? Greed. The fool sending me the email hopes I comply in claiming my winnings. Delete! When someone asks me about "419" letters or Nigerian fraud, I try to keep my calm while responding to their ignorance.

There is no doubt there are many Nigerian doings that need to be eradicated. The current President Yar'Adua seems to be the right person for those critical positive changes. I am asking that when people talk about Nigeria, please focus on the specific issue or person than generalize all Nigerians. Here is an example of what am asking. I visited Italy a few years ago. My family and I went from Rome to Napoli to Milano. If my money was not in my underwear, it would have been stolen. There were pick pockets everywhere. Yet people flock to Italy yearly with many more, myself included, enjoying Italian cuisine. Should I conclude that all Italians are thieves? Absolutely not! Will I visit Italy again? Absolutely Yes! Is there no corruption or scam in the U.S.? Watch Robert Greenwald's movie *"Wal-Mart: The High Cost of Low Price"* to see how Wal-Mart manipulates the system.

Now back to the Wal-Mart manager conversations.

After meeting with a number of managers, I decided it was best for our sanity to start with only two products even though four were approved. We would start with the best selling Jollof Rice and Sheba Stew. The managers where relieved when I informed them that I was starting with only two products. This meant less space for them to give up. At the end of the meetings with all the 29 managers, only 24 agreed to put the products in the store. The 1/3 of the struggle, LSQ application, was over. Now the 2/3 of keeping the products in the store began. The managers and I went over the supplier agreement that I signed, in regards to the product delivery and returns. They wanted to make sure I understood what was expected of me. The starting units for the Jollof Rice and Sheba Stew was 1152 units. The first orders required purchase order numbers, so the initial delivery was properly recorded in the Wal-Mart system. No purchase order numbers were required for subsequent orders. I was to visit the store at least once a week to gauge the product's movement.

PRODUCT PRODUCTION

In order for a company (co-packer) to produce my product, I had to release my formula and process. I struggled with this for weeks. What is to stop the co-packer from taking my market, once they see how profitable the product is? They also had the finances needed for marketing. There is a lot of stealing in the food industry. Someone said to me that if they wanted to know the exact ingredients in my product, all that's needed is to buy it from the store. Send it to a lab which would detail the ingredients. If their research and development team fail to perfect the product, they'll hire Africans to teach them what's needed. In the same breath, the person told me to make hay while the sun shines. The first entrant should set the bar of entry high enough to deter new entrants. Instead of worrying about someone stealing the product, I should focus on branding and marketing.

Eventually, I did release the formula and process to the co-packer. The first production was a disaster with a substantial amount lost. The Jollof Rice did not turn as well as when I produced it. In hindsight, it was encouraging that the product couldn't be easily duplicated. We worked things out for other productions.

MARKETING PLAN

One cannot put a product in the freezer, without marketing and expect it to sell. As I did the budget, I discovered there were no funds for marketing. It dawned on me that media needs content for news. In asking myself a series of questions, I got my solution. How many minority companies have products in Wal-Mart? A few. How many African companies sell products to major supermarkets, specifically food to Wal-Mart? None! That must be news worthy. I decided that getting my information to media, a zero cost, would be part of Sheba Foods' marketing plan. Publicity is always better than advertising for it gives credibility. At the end of the day, many notable media outlets wrote stories, did radio interviews or gave television exposure about Sheba Foods. All of which were valued at over $100,000. Many of the Sheba Foods' media exposure are listed on www.shebafoods.com/news.aspx. To God be the Glory! Wal-Mart benefited from Sheba Foods' exposure.

WAL-MART DELIVERY TIMES

Delivery days were generally Monday to Friday. A few stores receive products on Saturdays and Sundays. Delivery times starts from four a.m., ends between eight a.m. and eleven a.m. The Wal-Mart receivers were one of my favorites. I felt a wow factor from many of them. They had never had a minority food supplier deliver products. The frequent question I got was: How did you pass all of Wal-Mart's red tape? My answer: The Grace of God. A few would say Amen, while others simply smiled and shook their heads.

It sometimes took up to two hours for product delivery. Why? There were many deliveries within the limited receiving hours. Every unit of product, whether new or damaged, must be inputted into the Wal-Mart's computer system, and a report printed for each supplier. One delivery can be 100 cases, with the driver taking back cases of returns. Upon arrival, prior to the gates opening, there is no number to take. People eye marked who arrived after them. I tried to arrive first or second. Once the delivery door opened, I signed the receiving book. Got my badge and took the products to the designated store freezer. Once the store shelf is filled, the remaining products went into the storage freezer. I tried to not leave the products in the Wal-Mart storage freezer, because I don't know when they'll put the products out.

DELIVERY TO THE 24 STORES BEGAN

It was an overwhelming task plotting the delivery and demos for the 24 stores. I got serious headaches, insomnia and anxiety. The farthest store was in Warner Robbins, Georgia. I had to go to the plant which was 1.5 hours from my house. The travel time from the plant to Warner Robbins was four hours. Total travel time was 11 hours — 5.5 hours each way. That was the only delivery for that day.

I was glad that I personally delivered all first orders. A few took up to three hours. Many of the products would have been returned if someone else did the deliveries. There were issues with the purchase order numbers. Either they were not found in the system, or the receivers questioned their validity, even though there were in the system.

African food? The receivers sometimes would not accept the products unless the freezer manager was present. To resolve the purchase order number issues, I waited until the office that generated the number, called the UPC office, opened at seven a.m. or eight a.m. This was an issue in Warner Robbins, Macon and other far out stores. Leaving to come back was not an option; given my arrival was five a.m. I used the downtime to catch up on sleep. For the remaining stores, delivery was done when the UPC office was open, and frozen food manager on duty.

Knowing the manager's day off this early turned out to be an asset. It took about three weeks to deliver products to all the stores. A number of the stores did not put the products out for several weeks because the managers had no freezer space for them. For those who had space, I placed the products where directed and made sure the shelf price label was generated and in place before I left. The distance for a number of stores, made it necessary to conduct demos on delivery days. Demos were scheduled at the time of delivery and conducted when the manager was on duty. The manager witnessed our presence. This confirmed my marketing plan to the buyer was executed.

DELIVERY FIASCO AT THE GAINESVILLE STORE

I live in Georgia, considered the heart of the South and Slavery. This Gainesville experience proved that the more things change, the more they remain the same. The Gainesville store, the last store to give its order, was in the difficult food merchandiser's territory. Gainesville delivery time ends at eleven a.m. Prior to delivery, there was strong resistance at this store. I remember the day of delivery as if it was yesterday. It was a nasty heavy rain and thunderstorm day. I arrived at the Canton store at nine-thirty a.m. It was my second delivery of the day. I knew that I would not make it to Gainesville in time. Travel time from Canton to Gainesville was almost one hour. One of the best ways to annoy the receiving personnel and be blacklisted, is to arrive 15 minutes before closing time.

I called the Gainesville frozen food manager and told her that I was running late, and would most likely arrive after receiving had closed. The manager said to still come and she would receive the products it in the system herself. I would have delivered the product the next day, if she had said it was not okay to come that day. I called receiving to relate what the manager said. Receiving stated that as long as the manager okayed it, there was no problem.

I arrived at Gainesville after eleven a.m. I went to the back of the store because sometimes the receiving door stays open past receiving hours. The steel receiving door was down, locked. Drove to the front of the store and took the product through the front door. I asked for the frozen food manager. She was no where to be found, even after being paged several times. I put my products in the storage freezer. 45 minutes went by, no frozen food manager. I then asked for the Store Manager and was told he was out to lunch. Another 45 minutes went by, no frozen food manager, no store manager. I called a few friends on my cell phone to pass the time, relating what was happening at the Gainesville store. I was determined to not leave until I had seen the frozen food manager. It's now almost one p.m. I saw a group of managers, four to five, gathered talking, occasionally glancing in my direction. When they finished and dispersed, one walked to me. As he approached, I took deep breaths, asked God to let me utter the right words because I was really upset. I had been in the store for over two hours and both managers were missing. He asked: "How can I help you?" I looked at his badge and it said co-manager. I calmly related what happened and asked if the frozen food manager was now available.

He said no, she had to leave for the day. I asked if the Store Manager was available. He said: "Do you have an appointment?" I said no. He said: "How can you just walk up in here and demand to see the manager?" I explained that I did not plan on meeting with the Store Manager. It is in the absence of not seeing the freezer manager that prompted the desire to see the Store Manager. A manager needs to receive the product if receiving is closed. He asked what product I was delivering. I told him African food. He then told me that "they" had checked with the food merchandiser and he told them that they did not have to take my product. This was the food merchandiser that reluctantly signed my LSQ. His office was in the Gainesville store. I had two thoughts for this co-manager that I did not utter, but am sure the thoughts were written on my face.

1. Why did the frozen food manager place her order?

2. Why didn't she share this revelation when I spoke with her that morning?

I asked to speak with the food merchandiser since he was in the building. The co-manager got really upset. What he said next threw me off balance. He said: "You can't just walk up in here demanding attention; we are the highest generating Wal-Mart food store in all of Georgia. Take your f...ing product and get out of my store!" Right there in open store floor with customers and sales associates looking at us. I was dump founded, busted into tears, ran into the nearest bathroom and had a good cry. After I had settled down, I removed the products from the freezer. Left the store about two p.m.

While in the Gainesville parking lot and still in tears, I called Wal-Mart's Supplier Diversity department. The lady I spoke with was so sympathetic, she transferred me to Lee Scott's office (Wal-Mart's President). I was put on hold briefly and Mr. Scott's assistant came on line and asked for a detailed recap. I later wondered if she recorded the call and if legal was on line as I told the story. There was a long pause after I related what happened. She then asked what I considered a critical question. We knew this was an excellent opportunity for a lawsuit. She asked what I would like to see happen. I said that I had no plans of suing Wal-Mart. I told her that history was being made. African foods at Wal-Mart should generate good publicity for Wal-Mart. I continued that all I wanted was an opportunity to have a fair trial of my products in the stores they were approved for.

She said that the entire management team at the Gainesville store will be spoken to immediately, and to deliver the products the next day. I responded that in the light of what happened, I will remove the store from my list. She was okay with the decision. She asked how many remaining stores I had left to deliver to, I told her. She gave me the frozen foods VP's phone number. I am to call him should any issues arise with any other store, or call her back if needed. I did not call the VP. However, all the stores thereafter were nicer. The managers that had my products in the storage freezer for weeks, suddenly found space on the store freezer shelves.

All of the difficult food merchandiser's stores put the products in bad locations—on the top shelves which didn't have light, behind the hinge of the freezer door. You have to be looking for the products to find them. To fight back, I doubled demos for those stores. When I and my staff did demos, 12 to 24 units of products were sold within four hours. People liked the products. Unfortunately, there were minimal or no sales when we did not do demos. I had other stores to service and eventually cut back on the demos for those difficult stores.

WAL-MART'S RETAILLINK SYSTEM

Retaillink becomes relevant once deliveries are made. It allowed me to retrieve product sales data on a daily basis. Once a supplier is accepted, there is a Wal-Mart phone number to call which then gets the supplier setup in the Retaillink system. A username and password is issued. The system is quite complex. The online training was difficult to follow, despite my past experience of writing, teaching and troubleshooting software applications. It took me a month to learn the basics. The technical support staff made it clear that it was not their job to teach me or other suppliers how to use the system. Given my limited understanding of Retaillink, my reports produced errors. After numerous calls to Wal-Mart technical support, the reports were fixed. It was exciting viewing hourly products' movement in all the stores. The information guided my scheduling store demos. Retaillink was also great for tracking deliveries, returns, invoices, payment schedule and checks.

COST OF DEMOS AND THE EXPERIENCE

Demos are effective marketing tools in generating product sales. Doing store demos at Ingles and Wal-Mart confirmed this. Sales increased by 400%. I calculated the cost to hire one of Wal-Mart's approved demo companies. 24 stores x $150 (4-6 hour demo) = $3,600 x 4 weeks = $14,400/month. Out of my budget! How much sales can they guarantee for this investment? Zero. It was much cheaper for me to hire staff and do the demos. It was even cheaper when I did the demos personally, eliminated the staff cost.

My job requirements in hiring staff for the demos was simple: be clean, friendly, outspoken and professional. I and my staff welcomed every opportunity to educate people about African food. Many of the people who tried the product, were experiencing it for the first time. It was truly a joy watching them enjoy both products. Comments were "it tastes good...a bit spicy...not spicy enough....it tastes like Jambalaya" etc. We sampled when people were hungry, when there were shopping to cook a meal. Our product was easy, heat and serve. During the weekdays, the demo time was four p.m. — seven p.m., and on weekends 12 noon — eight p.m.

There were many reasons why I loved doing demos. One was recruitment of good demo sales personnel met in the stores. Another was that people gave great advice for product improvement, marketing techniques and helped get media exposure for Sheba Foods. We kept a number of the products next to us, in the open Wal-Mart freezer, for customers who wished to buy after tasting. Saturdays were my favorite demo days because other company products were being demoed. The rows of tables with various foods and drinks were a welcome attraction for the customers. I sometimes bartered my products; had great lunches or dinners and took extras home. At the end, I bought many of the other products I tasted. Whenever possible, I asked the Juice or Chicken demo person to set up next to me. We complemented each other. The demo people and I became such good friends we sent tasters to each other's tables.

THINGS USED FOR OUR DEMOS

I had to be creativity with my tight budget in having a professional presentation. Utilized skills acquired earlier in life in making an effective presentation.

1. *4 to 6 foot table*—We started out with different tables which did not meet my needs. After a few demos, I designed and personally built functional and professional tables out of 4 x 8 1/4inch wood sheets and PVC (plastic) 10 foot pipes.

2. *Table cover* — bought enough $1 per yard imitation African fabric from an outlet store. Sowed covers with overlaps, creating curtain effects for the tables.

3. *Microwave* — a small unit. I went to many thrift stores and bought numerous microwaves for $10 or less, versus $60+ for a new one.

4. *Microwavable containers* — to heat the frozen product. Part of the demonstration was to show the ease of frozen to hot.

5. *2 oz cups* — ensured a good size portion was given for a taste, hoping the taster wants more and buys at least one unit. It worked many times.

6. *Napkins* — came in handy for the customer and us in cleaning spills.

7. *Spoons* — for both the Jollof Rice and Sheba Stew.

8. *Door Signs* — I designed signs that stated: "Join us for Exotic African Cuisine on Aisle Two. Products being sampled: Jollof Rice and Sheba Stew." Taped signs on Wal-Mart entry doors.

9. *Flyers* — usually 4 x 6 printed off my inkjet color printer. Our current postcards are professionally printed on card stock glossy paper.

10. *Questionnaires* — One of the most important things that we handed out to those who tasted the food was a questionnaire. It was my way of knowing how many people stopped by my staff's table and their response to the products.

11. *Waste basket* — this is the only thing I did not have to buy or bring. Used those in the Wal-Mart stores.

Chapter Four

The Process for the Jollof Rice Deli Entry

The greater the difficulty,
the more glory in surmounting it.
Skillful pilots gain their reputations
from storms and tempests.
Epictetus

DECISION TO ENTER DELI

I think of the deli as the fast food outlet which happens to be in a supermarket. Who cooks from scratch in America? Everyone is so busy, giving eateries reasons to thrive. The deli is excellent exposure and volume for any of its retail products. In most supermarkets, it has the highest food sales, and offers the supplier higher profit margins with virtually zero returns. Doing demos planted the idea of food service, which resulted in the production of 5-pound Jollof Rice bags and 1-gallon Sheba Stews. I felt the Jollof Rice would do well in the deli, where it can be served hot with the chicken offerings. That feeling was supported by two of Wal-Mart's food merchandisers. One of them stated that they've been asking Wal-Mart to add rice and no one listened. In addition to the reasons already stated, my deli entry eliminated these issues with the freezer products:

1. Poor product placement in the freezer.

2. High production and delivery costs.

3. High demo expenses—fewer demos needed since customers asked the deli sales associates for samples.

GETTING READY FOR DELI ENTRY

It had been six months since the 16-ounce Jollof Rice debuted in the freezer. Time to exercise Wal-Mart's policy of adding new products and stores. One of the wonderful things about a growing company is the ability to make quick product development decisions. I had to quickly decide the packaging for the 5-pound bag. I called eight plastic companies. Got samples of plastic bags for testing. The bag needed to remain stable from packing to freezing to reheating. After many trials with various bags, I choose two. Despite all the tests, upon delivery to the Wal-Mart deli, there were instances were the rice bags opened in the steamer. We tried different bags in an attempt to fix the issue. Looking back, I should have found out the Wal-Mart steamer's temperature and gotten bags that could withstand their steam.

The Nutrition Facts is the same for both sizes, however, serving per container for the 16-ounce is two (2).

Cooking directions below are for the 5-pound bag. For 16-ounce container - open, put lid back on, microwave for eight minutes and serve.

Cooking Directions:

Warmer   Place in warmer/steamer until warm or hot. Serve.

Microwave Put holes in the bag before putting in microwave.
          Heat on high until hot.
          (appr. 20 minutes depending on temperature)

Oven   Heat oven to 300° (degrees). Pour contents in pan & cover.
       Heat for 1 hour or desired temperature. Stir every 25 minutes.

Jollof Rice ideas shown on the Recipe Page on
www.shebafoods.com

Nutrition Facts

Serving Size 1 cup (225g/8oz)
Serving Per Container - 10

Amount/serving		
Calories 330 Calories from Fat 120		
		% Daily Value*
Total Fat 13g		20%
Saturated Fat 2g		9%
Cholesterol 0mg		0%
Sodium 560mg		23%
Total Carborhydrate 48g		16%
Dietary Fiber 4g		15%
Sugars 4g		
Protein 5g		

Vitamin A 15%	•	Vitamin C 4%
Calcium 2%	•	Iron 20%

*Percent Daily Values are based on a 2,000 calorie diet. Your daily values may be higher or lower depending on your calorie needs:

		Calories:	2,000	2,500
Total Fat		Less than	65g	80g
Saturated Fat		Less than	20g	25g
Cholesterol		Less than	300mg	300mg
Sodium		Less than	2,400mg	2,400mg
Total Carbohydrate			300g	375g
Dietary Fiber			25g	30g

Calories per gram:
    Fat 9 • Carbohydrate 4 • Protein 4

Given the anticipated volume, I decided it would be more efficient to outsource the production to a co-packer. I found a company that had the setup needed, did not make a similar product nor had the desire to make a similar product.

GETTING SIGNATURES AGAIN — RESISTANCE AND APPROVAL

To my knowledge, in 2004, there were no minorities selling products to any Wal-Mart deli. All the products were from non-minority companies, large corporations. The two food merchandisers who gladly signed for the freezer products, signed again for the deli, giving me 31 stores. I had to go back to the difficult food merchandiser whose home store was the Gainesville store. I needed his stores because a number them were high volume earners and closest to my house. He commented that he was shocked that the products were approved for the freezer. He refused to sign this time, felt his signature would be a waste, even if the District Manager and God himself signed. He went on to add that the buyer will not approve this questionnaire.

I could not remember when I slept well last. I had been exceptionally stressed and done all that was in my power. My husband had the pressure of house bills and was not supportive at all of the Wal-Mart entry. He told me to quit Wal-Mart and get a job so I can help with the bills. He added: "Afterall, you have two degrees, use it!" I thought I was. I cried buckets. I was all alone. Will I let those who gave me condolences on my Wal-Mart entry win? Absolutely not! Prayer is generally what one does as a last resort. This was as good a time as any to talk to God. I laid on my face. Prayed that my husband would have patience with me as I built Sheba Foods. Psalm 35 became my mantra for the food merchandiser. I fell in love with the first paragraph: "Contend Oh Lord with X (the food merchandiser), as he contends with me...." Translated: "Big Daddy, get the bully." I phoned the difficult food merchandiser repeatedly the following weeks. I left a message each time, stating I would appreciate him changing his mind, that I had three young children to support and needed this Wal-Mart business. He did not return a single call. I refused to send the two signed questionnaire to Bentonville. After all, I had 31 stores, most people would be happy with that. It was all or nothing for me. Even though I had the Wal-Mart frozen food VP's phone number, I did not use it. Why? He was not over deli. I could have called Lee Scott's assistant, but did not.

Then on one glorious day, one of the two friendlier food merchandisers called. He had taken over the difficult food merchandiser's territory and would be glad to sign for the 14 stores if I still desired it. Halleluyah!! At the end, all the stores were approved, giving me 45 stores! My freezer application for the Brunswick Stew and Pork Barbecue was also approved for 45 stores. The difficult food merchandiser was not fired, just re-assigned. Thank you Jesus!

WAL-MART'S DIVERSITY PHILOSOPHY

The Wal-Mart website states that "diversity is a key dimension of their commitment to customers, suppliers, and associates. To treat them with fairness and respect, be their advocates, be sensitive to their concerns, value their differences, and serve and support them the best we can." Did Wal-Mart practice this diversity philosophy in my

Deli Jollof Rice Approval Letter

WALMART Stores Inc.

Corporate Offices
702 S. W. 8th St.
Bentonville, AR 72716-0145

Confidential information
such as buyer's name and
contact information has
been deleted to protect
buyer's identity.

Sheba Foods

Dear Kunmi Oluleye:

Enclosed you will find a Wal-Mart Stores, Inc. **Supplier Agreement and Addendum**. This Agreement will need to be completed according to the instructions on the Supplier Agreement Form.

Please complete all other pertinent forms enclosed and return the completed items to:

> Wal-Mart Stores, Inc.
> Bentonville, AR 72716-0145

As soon as we receive the correctly completed and signed Supplier Agreement, Wal-Mart will be able to assign the appropriate vendor number.

You will be authorized to sell **only** the **item or items submitted on this Questionnaire**. Local Purchase is store specific and Item(s) specific. Approved item(s): **Jollof Rice for Deli** Dpt 80/93/97

Additional items or expansion into more stores will need **prior written approval** by submitting a new questionnaire, which has been signed by a store manager and district manager/ food merchandiser (food Items) to the Local Purchase Department.   Testing (if needed) will be completed through local purchases and buyer approval will be obtained. A **six month** sales history will be required before submitting additional requests.

We request that you <u>do not deliver</u> to any Wal-Mart store until we contact you with your supplier number. You will then be authorized to sell to the following stores .

> District # 120, 467, 515, 449, 231, 319, 515, 903, 140
> Store # 594, 745, 1367, 273, 1121, 1143, 1024, 1340, 1076, 2890, 1153, 1314, 3462, 3205, 494, 878, 1112, 1047, 3201, 2475, 548, 1400, 1184, 1373, 2941, 1586, 3461, 932, 1578, 1720, 5252, 1488, 1586, 3205, 615, 618, 669, 856, 1070, 1215, 1488, 1586, 2732, 3205, 34

Failure to comply with the above restrictions will result in your supplier number being revoked immediately.

Sincerely,

Brunswick Stew & Pork Barbecue Approval Letter

WAL-MART
Corporate Offices
702 S W 8th Street
Bentonville, AR 72716-0145
6/21/05

Sheba Foods

Dear Kunmi Oluleye:

Enclosed you will find the Wal-Mart Stores, Inc. Supplier Agreement with the appropriate signatures. Your Supplier Number is   selling merchandise in ***Department 91.***

NOTE: Local Purchase is Item Specific and Store Specific! The store manager and district manager have been notified of your number and their ability to do business with you at this time. When you make shipments to the stores, please take a copy of this letter for verification of authorization. You must obtain a purchase order from the store prior to making ANY shipments. You should provide the store(s) with an invoice per store so the order may be paid by the store(s) you are servicing. Your check will come from home office. DO NOT SEND INVOICE TO HOME OFFICE!

 You are authorized to sell only the item or items listed on your Local Supplier Questionnaire with authorization to sell in
District # 120, 467, 515, 449, 231, 319, 515, 903, 140
Store(s) # 594, 745, 1367, 273, 1121, 1143, 1024, 1340, 1076, 2890, 1153, 1314, 3462, 3205, 494, 878, 1112, 1047, 3201, 2475, 548, 1400, 1184, 1373, 2941, 1586, 3461, 932, 1578, 1720, 5252, 1488, 1586, 3205, 615, 618, 669, 856, 1070, 1215, 1488, 1586, 2732, 3205, 34
Approved Item(s): Brunswick Stew, Port Barbeque-Jolif Rice for Deli IS NOT APPROVED

The Buyers Dept. will contact you with the items and
dates for delivery to store(s).

Failure to comply with the above restrictions will result in your supplier number being revoked immediately.

Please forward a copy of your Certificate of Insurance renewal when your policy has been renewed. Our files need to be kept current with this information.

A questionnaire requesting additional districts or stores will not be considered until a six months sales record can be submitted for review by the buyer with the questionnaire. Date for beginning to keep sales history is the date your company was assigned a vendor number through Local Purchases. You may not sell to any other store not listed on this letter without home office approval.

Sincerely

Supplier Development

Jollof Rice entry into the deli? Decide at the end of this Chapter.

PROJECTED DELI SALES

To estimate the number of bags the Wal-Mart deli would use per day, I asked the deli managers how much mashed potatoes they use daily. I also called fast food restaurants for their rice consumption. Before I could decide the Jollof Rice deli production, I had to consider the number of hours the Georgia Wal-Mart deli was open. Approximately ten hours a day, seven days a week. Assuming no sales for one day, that is a total of 60 hours possible per week. Also assuming they'll have the rice available for sale seven hours per day (deducted three hours for replenishing). That left 42 hours of potential sales per store, per week.

If Wal-Mart sells 1 to 1.25 pounds per hour, of course we know they should sell more, that translated to approximately 42 to 52 pounds of rice per week per store—8 to 10 bags—360 to 450 bags per week. For confidentiality, the numbers shown in the table fall within my projections. The last column sales are if the stores use 16 to 20 bags, instead of projected 8 to 10 bags. Using the numbers below, imagine sales when the product goes national with delivery to 3,000 stores. This is how millionaires are born in the deli, the reason why I insisted on 45 stores.

Projected Store Sales	Conservative weekly	Conservative Monthly	Conservative Year 1	Conservative Year 1 x2
Delivery to 5 stores	$1,800	$7,200	$86,400	$172,800
Delivery to 45 stores	$16,200	$64,800	$777,600	$1,555,200

I received the deli and freezer approval letters in the same month, a year apart, March 2004 and 2005. Both times, the freezer products (Jollof Rice, Sheba Stew, Brunwick Stew and Pork Barbecue) were built into the Wal-Mart system within two months. Why two months? A product id needed to be assigned to the UPC barcodes that I submitted. This is how the register knows to accept and checkout the product when scanned, so the customer can pay for it. Payment instructions needed to be setup to correlate with returns. The Wal-Mart system deducts monies due Wal-Mart (from returns) before supplier payment is issued. Retaillink authorization for Sheba Foods needed to be created.

By June 2005, the Brunswick Stew and Pork Barbecue for the freezer had been built into the system. This meant that I could begin to take the managers orders and deliver the products. I wondered why the deli Jollof Rice was not in the system. I called Supplier Diversity several times to find out the delay. They responded that the buyer was on vacation, in meetings or out in the field. Another month went by. I decided that desperate times required desperate measures. I remembered a discussion in one of my MBA classes about corporate board members. Have you ever

wondered why companies have board members? They are
selected for their race, gender, experience, exposure and
most importantly influence. Many times board members
use their influence to help the companies they represent.
Who were Wal-Mart's board members? Interestingly
enough, they were listed on the Wal-Mart website and one
of them was in Atlanta. Thank God for the internet. Later
that day, I attended an event where I complained about
Wal-Mart. One person said, "Do you know that Mr. Daft,
ex-President of Coca-Cola is one of the board members and
he is here in Atlanta?" "Really," I responded. That was my
confirmation that I should contact Mr. Daft.

The person went on to say, that Wal-Mart just added
an African-American man to their board and to explore that
angle as well. It was good to know that Wal-Mart had an
African-American on their board. Time was of the essence.
I had confirmation for Daft and went with it. The next
morning, I called Coca-Cola for Mr. Daft. Even though he
was no longer the Coca-Cola President, he still had an office
at Coca-Cola. His assistant related that he was vacationing
in Europe. I told her that I am a Wal-Mart supplier with
issues about Wal-Mart and needed his help dearly.

Within 24 hours, I got a call from Wal-Mart's legal.
"Ms. Oluleye, this is Robert Newell, ... I'll like to see how
I can help you?" "Wow! Counselor", I responded
".....thanks for your prompt response." Prior to the call
to Mr. Daft, I bought Pepsi's products. Given Mr. Daft's
help, my household became Coca-Cola consumers and we
still are. Occasionally buying Pepsi's products. I later
learned that Coca-Cola is one of the best companies to work
for. It treats its employees and suppliers with respect,
embracing diversity in the continents it operates in. Here

Mr. Robert J. Newell
Walmart Legal
702 S.W. 8th Street
Bentonville, AR 72716

September 2005
Response to WalMart letter
dated 8/31/05

Dear Mr. Newell:

I am in receipt of your letter dated August 31, 2005. I still want Walmart to move forward to try the Jollof Rice in the deli for the 45 stores listed in the approval letter that I received. The reason stated is not a rational basis for the buyer's decision. To my knowledge, Walmart has never tried rice in the deli even though a few deli managers have requested it. The managers do not agree with not being able to keep the rice in a satisfactory condition for their customers. The rice is more stable than the mash potatoes and macaroni & cheese Walmart deli currently offers. More stable because of the seasonings and method of preparation. Africans are the authors of preservation and our foods do not lend themselves to the bacteria that affect other cuisines. A sample of the Jollof Rice was sent to the buyers last year for testing. The market is definitely there because rice is generally served with chicken. An example is Publix's hot deli or Popeyes.

Additionally, the reason stated that the Jollof Rice is not being put in the deli because it is not selling well in the freezer is comparing apples to oranges. These are the questions that I previous asked, which has gotten no response:
1. Is the mashed potatoes that is sold in the deli sold in the freezer? If no, why not?
2. Is the smoked turkey drumsticks sold in selected delis sold in the freezer? If no, why not?

Different products do well in different markets and location. Answering those questions will show that the buyer has no rational basis for the decision to not put the Jollof Rice in the deli. A rational basis would be my race and/or gender.

WALMART'S DIVERSITY PROGRAM
It would seem that Walmart's diversity program accepts minority vendors to put on a good face, with the hope that they fail and actively puts systems in place that makes sure that they don't succeed. If Walmart is truly committed to diversity and helping a small business grow, it failed to show that in my case. What is the retention rate of minority vendors who had the opportunity to sell in Walmart? Why did they fail or was their vendor number withdrawn by Walmart?

For the letter from Walmart to say "Jollof Rice approved for deli", it means that the managers feel the product is good enough to try and signed the necessary papers showing their desire to have the product in their stores. One food merchandiser sign up over 30 stores for the Jollof Rice.

5295 Highway 78, D-110
Stone Mountain, Georgia 30087
Phone / Fax: 770-982-1000

Please visit us at: www.shebafoods.com
Email: hamni@shebafoods.com

In the last few weeks, I have gotten numerous credit memos from Walmart about my freezer products reported as damaged. This is harassment. These products are being maliciously destroyed and credit requested. I could have been called to pick up the products and issue a credit. This is not the first time that I will be harassed by Walmart management. I reported it to senior Walmart management, please see a copy of one letter. As a child of God, I cannot and will not be intimidated no matter what Walmart does.

USING WALMART'S NAME

My emailing my subscribers and media was to (1) show how progressive Walmart is in putting African cuisine in their stores (2) inform the public as to which Walmart stores they can purchase my products. Walmart has benefited positively since my products debut: (A) My webpage www.shebafoods.com/news.aspx lists a few of the media publicity. (B) My book "Selling my food to Supermarkets, Distributors, Etc." ISBN 0965480100 talks about Walmart in a positive light, but does mention the name. There is a sequel in progress.

How is a small business to promote their product to generate sales in your stores, if not able to say "available in these Walmarts"? This can be considered as one of those systems for failure of a small business within Walmart.

CONCLUSION

If Walmart's goal is generating revenue, offering great products to its customers, and having small and/or minority business thrive, then Walmart needs to try the Jollof Rice in the deli per the approval letter that I received. Walmart has done well in trying it in the freezer, please try it in the deli. Let's focus on making money and having great lasting relationships.

Please feel free to call me on my cell   . I look forward to your response.

Sincerely,
Kunmi Oluleye

5295 Highway 78, D-110   Please visit us at: www.shebafoods.com
Stone Mountain, Georgia 30087   Email: kunmi@shebafoods.com
Phone / Fax: 770-982-4000

Sept. 2005   b. 2 of 2   Response to Walmart letter dated 8/31/05 is Mr. Daft not on the same continent with me, getting me a total stranger, the attention I needed. Up to the publishing of this book, I had not met or spoken with Mr. Daft. See what happens when I called Ambassador Young (in Atlanta) and Mr. Jesse Jackson (in Chicago). For the record, Mr. Daft is white. Most people know Ambassador Young, but not all know Mr. Jackson, both men are African-Americans.

I gave Attorney Newell the details he wanted. He promised to get back with me soon. It was a pleasant conversation. Then I received a letter from him with bad news, dated August 31, 2005. Unfortunately, I can't share his letter. You can guess its content in my response. Before he sent the letter, he called to inform me of the letter's content which I thought was nice. On the phone and in the letter, he explained that Wal-Mart had tried rice in the deli and it failed. Prior to my conversation with Attorney Newell, I had called all 45 stores letting them know the Jollof rice was coming. When I asked how much mashed potatoes they sold, I also asked if they've ever offered rice. They all answered no, they've never served rice.

I was reminded to not use Wal-Mart's name anywhere to promote my products. My guess is that the attorney and Wal-Mart personnel had been on the Sheba Foods website and saw all 45 stores listed. Attorney Newell told me that I was in violation of my supplier agreement by having Wal-Mart listed on my site. I couldn't find the violation in my Wal-Mart agreement. How is the public to know where to buy my product if I don't tell them? Wal-Mart should be paying me for telling people to go there and buy my products. Whenever I go into a supermarket to buy one item, I buy numerous unplanned items. When people

SHEBA FOODS
FAX

Date: October 26, 2005

To: XXXXXXXX

From: Kunmi Oluleye

Re: Walmart Deli for Jollof Rice

Pages: 1 including this one

_____

Hello XXXXXX:

Thank you for the decision to move forward with the Jollof Rice. I really appreciate it. I need your help in deciding which 5 delis to start in. The idea is to pick 5 stores in Georgia with the highest hot deli sales. Please rank the stores listed below in order of sales, from highest to lowest. If you know of stores with higher sales not listed, please include them in your response.

Potential Stores:

1340	Lithonia
1047	Morrow
2154	Pleasant Hill
1578	Roswell
1488	Douglasville
1184	Stone Mountain
787	Riverdale
594	Fayetteville
3205	Lithia Springs

Please feel free to contact me with any questions at the office 770.982.1000, cell phone or email   @shebafoods.com. Thanks for your attention.

Sincerely,
Kunmi Oluleye

went to Wal-Mart for my products, they most likely bought other products Wal-Mart sold. Wal-Mart benefited from the perception that they've embraced diversity by stocking African products. The goodwill they gained was priceless.

I thank God for the absence of fear. I was perfectly comfortable writing all the letters sent, and conversations with Wal-Mart attorneys. What was there to lose? In my letters, I asked a lot of questions which till the publishing of this book were not answered. Shortly after sending the letters, I began getting memos that the unexpired, recently delivered freezer products were now damaged. My supplier agreement specified that I was to physically handle the damaged products, exercising one of two options (a) replace with new ones, no credit (b) issue credit (refund). Many times during my deliveries, I witnessed drivers from other companies pick up their damage products, and replaced it with new ones. Both the Wal-Mart receiver and driver counted the products together. A report was then generated by Wal-Mart receiving to confirm the delivery and returns. The alleged damaged products did not match up with our deliveries and inventory shown in Retaillink. Moreover, I didn't get a chance to see the "damaged" products, yet asked to reimburse Wal-Mart. How do I know that the amount requested was right? It didn't matter. I had to pay the large amount Wal-Mart dictated to me. This was harassment. They tried to frustrate my freezer efforts, hoping I'll get upset and quit. I communicated to Wal-Mart's management that was sabotage of Sheba Foods' Wal-Mart survival.

In October 2005, I got 10% victory. The buyer decided to move forward with only five stores for a 90-day deli trial. I was to pick any five stores anywhere Wal-Mart operated. I was not confined to Georgia even though my approval letter specifically stated only Georgia stores. I knew it was a trick. The stores definitely had to be in Georgia. It would be more difficult and financially involved to service stores out of Georgia. I was not happy with the five stores but decided that 10% of bread is better than none.

This next Wal-Mart move was clever. In November 2005, I was told that prior to moving forward with the five stores, I needed a new Supplier Evaluation Report from D & B. The D & B's rating scale is 1 to 9. The buyer told me that if the rating is 7 or more our relationship would be over. I was not worried. I expected the rating to be much lower than 7. No one at Wal-Mart asked me to pull a new D & B Supplier Evaluation Report for the Brunswick Stew and Pork Barbecue that was submitted and approved at the same time. If the Supplier Evaluation Report was not requested for the freezer products, why request it for the deli product? The answer from Wal-Mart was that they just needed it.

THE DUN & BRADSTREET (D & B) CONTRIBUTION

I paid the D & B $75 fee. 10 days later the Supplier Evaluation Report showed a 9. The worst possible rating it could be. I was stunned! I took deep breaths, reminded myself that as an overcomer, I will never turn my back on a battle and run. I asked the D & B representative to please fax the names of the companies reporting negatively, so I can address the issue that was causing the horrible rating. She said no. I asked why. She said it was D & B's policy to not release the companies' identity for privacy reasons. That made no sense to me. I told the Wal-Mart D & B woman about the TV advertisements in which people

Errorenous Report   SUPPLIER EVALUATION   For the Jollof Rice
                                                Deli Entry

DUNS: DATE PRINTED: SUMMARY
                          NOV 21 2005   =======

IROK SOLUTIONS INC   CONTROL   2000
  +SHEBA FOODS   SALES $500,000
                                      EMPLOYS   2 TOTAL

                                      PRIMARY SIC NO. 2038
                                      MFG ETHNIC FOODS

CHIEF EXECUTIVE: KUNMI OLULEYE,
                 PRESIDENT

                    SUPPLIER RISK SCORE FOR THIS FIRM = 9

SUPPLIER RISK SCORE

          Lowest Risk   Highest Risk

               1   2   3   4   5   6   7   8 < 9 >

The Supplier Risk Score predicts the likelihood of a firm ceasing
business without paying all creditors in full, or reorganising or
obtaining relief from creditors under state/federal law over the next
12 months. The score was calculated using a statistically valid model
derived from D&B's extensive data files.

                    INCIDENCE OF FINANCIAL STRESS

The Incidence of Financial Stress is the proportion of firms with scores
in this range that discontinued operations with loss to creditors.
Based on historical data in Dun & Bradstreet's files, the Incidence of
Financial Stress over the past year was as follows:

    INCIDENCE OF FINANCIAL STRESS: 35.80%   (3580 PER 10,000)
    - Supplier Risk Score of 9

    INCIDENCE OF FINANCIAL STRESS: 1.40%   (140 PER 10,000)
    - National Average

                    SUPPLIER RISK SCORE ANALYSIS

KEY FINANCIAL COMMENTARY:
    - Payment experiences exist for this firm which are greater than 60 days
      past due.
    - 57% of trade experiences indicate slow payment(s) are present.
    - No record of open suit(s), lien(s), or judgement(s) in the D&B files.
    - Payment information indicates negative payment comments.
    - Control age or date entered in D&B files indicates higher risk.

RISK COMMENTARY
    - Average Payments are more than 120 days beyond terms.

stated: "....it was stated in D & B, that's why they made the credit decisions..." The woman was quiet. I questioned the validity of all D & B reports given what was happening to me.

I asked for her manager. She stated it was her and one other woman. I'll call the first woman, Woman 1 and the second woman, Woman 2. It felt like a very bad dream. I told both women that if my individual credit report showed negative reporting, the contact information of the company would be listed. I have the option to correct the negative information. Both got upset with me. Woman 1 stated that she understood my being upset, for it meant that my relationship with Wal-Mart was terminated. She continued that she had other calls waiting and needed to go. I asked her to have Woman 2 call me, maybe I could communicate better with her. Woman 2 repeated the exact thing Woman 1 said, and was not nice at all about it. Apparently, they've discussed my report. She felt enough explanation was given, and was not going to keep repeating herself.

One of the dynamics that I've dealt with having a foreign (African) name, is that people think I don't understand English. Another is that many people feel that Africans are stupid because they speak differently. I consistently have to educate people that Africa is a continent and not a country. I know that am speaking to an enlightened person if he or she relates the travel to the continent by saying: "I went to Nigeria, Ghana or name the African country," adding the region in Africa, instead of "I went to Africa." I felt these women saw me as a stupid African and decided to play the part.

I called back and told Woman 1 that given that I am

from Africa, English is not my first language. I would appreciate it if they could put their reasoning on paper and fax it to me. I can then get someone who understands English, to interpret for me so that I better understand their position. Woman 1 declined. She said my English sounded fine to her. If I had that letter, I would have included it in this book to further support my point. The D & B executives reading this will have no doubt these conversations happened. I called the buyer and he expressed disappointment as to not continuing with the Jollof Rice in the deli because of the D & B report. I felt he smiled as he hung up the phone. Oh boy! They had won. I felt raped by Wal-Mart through D & B. The tears just kept rolling.

Who can I call? I called D & B's main office only to be directed back to the Wal-Mart's dedicated D & B's women whom I've already spoken with. I called friends who were business executives and used D & B. They had never had this happen and more importantly were shocked that D & B did not reveal the names of the companies so I could address it.

I paced back and forth for a while, could not sleep that day. Something was wrong, and I had no clue how to fix it. How do you fight an invisible enemy? I began to wonder if Voodoo was at work. That would explain all that was happening. My husband was glad the Wal-Mart relationship was over, now Kunmi will have to get a job. He offered no suggestions nor was sympathetic. After a few days of such misery, it occurred to me one morning that there was one more person that I needed to call. JESUS!!! It was a wireless call with no phone charges. I spent a few days on my face talking to Jesus, His Father the Almighty God and the Holy Spirit. I didn't make any promises. Many people when in a place of desperation like I was, make promises. God if you do this for me, I'll do X Y and Z. I simply asked God to show Himself strong on my behalf and I'll give him the Glory. It is time again for Daddy to beat up the bully.

Many Christians at this point would say that it is the lack of my church attendance, or not paying tithes that resulted in all the trouble. If I were to list all the miracles God had done in my life over the last four years, it would fill a book. I disagree that my dis-association with the Church prompted what was happening. Why does God keep showing up when I petition Him? He knows I love him and we talk regularly, not just in Church or with His saints. When I did go to Church and paid tithes, I paid more than 10%, so the reserve covered the last four years.

I was in deep depression for days after my conversation with the D & B women. I did not take a bath, nor ate for I had no appetite. I discovered that it takes over a week for one to die from lack of food and drink. I was a mess. My husband did a great job taking care of the kids.

My basement floor and I had become best friends. Such best friends that I placed the coach's seats on the floor to soften the concrete I tend to fall onto. While in deep depression, after petitioning the Trinity, I wrote a letter to the buyer stating that I KNOW that there is a great mistake with the D & B report. I went on to say that when the mistake is cleared up, the five stores that he had offered me will no longer be acceptable given all Wal-Mart was doing to frustrate the process. I stated that I expect to deliver to all 45 stores. He did not respond. I assumed his response was "in your dreams Kunmi, ..."

I had a horrible Thanksgiving. For those who don't know, it is an American holiday that is celebrated the last Thursday in November. What was there to be thankful for? In hindsight, there was a lot. I am blessed with three very healthy, intelligent and great looking children. I had a roof over my head. Three meals if I wanted. Even though my husband was not supportive of Sheba Foods, he paid the bills which allowed me to focus on Sheba Foods. I had a lot to be thankful for.

A week after the last conversation with the Wal-Mart D & B women, I called to see if there was a change in status to my Supplier Evaluation Report. Woman 1 put me on hold, came back and said there had been a change. My heart beated faster. I knew the report couldn't get any worse. She said the rating was now a 3 ....YES!!!!!!! I screamed Halleluyah in her ears, clapping my hands at the same time. I then asked if she could share the companies that gave the negative report. She still would not tell me. What does it matter now? Woman 1 told me that the updated Supplier Evaluation Report was sent to the buyer two days earlier. Why did they not call me given how we left the conversation? She stated that they had a lot of suppliers to process and it is not their procedure to call suppliers. Their communication is limited to Wal-Mart personnel. At last, this D & B experience was over.

One page of the several pages of the Supplier Evaluation Report is shown. The rating shown is within these brackets < >. In this erroneous report it was a 9. As of August 2007, our D & B rating is a two (2).

BUYER MOVES ON WITH RICE TRIAL

I did not call the buyer after I hung up with the D & B woman. I took a long hot bath. Cooked, ate, hugged my kids and went to sleep. I must have slept for over 12 hours!

Chapter Five

The 90-Day Jollof Rice Trial

If at first you don't succeed,
destroy all evidence that you tried.
Susan Ohanian

I called the buyer during the first week of December 2005. Left a message that I was ready to move on with the 45 stores. It was a great feeling! Many times when I wondered where God was for he just seemed to be napping on my issues. The D & B situation was an undisputable example of His power. How does a rating go from nine to three? I wished He would show up prior to my going into deep depression. As I wrote this preceding sentence, a thought came to me: *"It is the only time I get your full attention, Kunmi. It's the only time you spend time with me as I need you to..."* No response from buyer throughout December 2005.

From January to February 2006, I called and emailed the buyer repeatedly and did not get a single response. I wanted to start the trial in December 2005 because it was the height of the holiday shopping season. The first stop for hungry shoppers' especially children is the hot deli. Studies show that 40% of U.S. retail sales happen between November and December. I knew Wal-Mart would have five times its regular traffic, giving serious exposure to the Jollof Rice. The long lines meant that the customers were looking into the glass case where the rice was displayed. Chances are they would want to sample, then buy it.

I needed data of the highest Georgia Wal-Mart delis. The buyer refused to give the needed data which would have helped in selecting the trial stores. From the outburst of the Gainesville manager, I knew Gainesville was one of them, but was not going back there. I made a list of the Wal-Mart stores with high sales for the freezer Sheba Stew and Jollof Rice. I had an idea which store was busier, but needed confirmation. I went into the Wal-Mart stores, asked associates and managers to help rate the stores. I would say: "Between your store, X, Y and Z, which is busier?"

While waiting for the buyer to move forward with the deli rice, I focused my energy on doing demos. An effort to continue selling the products in the freezer. This was an opportunity to announce its debut in the deli. I didn't have to pitch the five managers to put the product in their delis. They had been briefed. All I had to do was show up and take their orders. Then trouble began. One by one, my five high sales stores had an excuse. The Lithonia store told me they had no warmer and therefore could not be part of the five stores. The substitutions of the stores was frustrating.

In March 2006, there was still no response from the buyer even after I faxed him the list of stores desired. One store took delivery despite the rice code was not built into the computer system. They couldn't sell it and kept it in the freezer. I decided that if communicating with one board member got a 24-hour response, communicating with 14 should get faster response. Two of the 14 board members were Wal-Mart President Lee Scott and Wal-Mart Chairman. The list of board members on Wal-Mart's website did not include phone numbers. It took over two weeks for me to get the phone and fax numbers. Late one night, I faxed my letter to all them.

The next morning, my phone rang continuously. A call from Wal-Mart legal, the buyer, supplier diversity, people who knew I was faxing the letter and wanted to see if there has been a response. I was on the phone for most of the day. Legal assured me that we are moving forward with the five stores. I told legal that I would be coming back for the remaining 40 stores after the 90-day trial. Buyer promised that the product would be built in the system for all the stores within two days and it was. I can't remember what Supplier Diversity wanted.

DELIVERIES & DEMOS

By early May 2006, the five stores which were relatively close to me, had taken delivery. The Lithonia store got a warmer and was part of the five trial stores. The farthest store was one hour away. All deliveries were done on the weekday when the managers were present. The stores did not put the rice out when it was delivered for two reasons:

March 28, 2006

Letter sent to All (14)
Wal-Mart Board Members

Dear Board Member:

I'll like to share with you my vendor experience with Wal-Mart and I need your help with the current problem that I am having. IROK Solutions, Inc. dba Sheba Foods is a certified Women Business Enterprise (WBE) and Minority Business Enterprise (MBE) company. We are the First and Only Manufacturer of Fresh Frozen and Packaged Authentic African Cuisine in the World. Our products are all natural and non-genetically modified.

For food products, please visit www.shebafoods.com/products.aspx. Our goal is to economically empower the African continent by generating American consumers interest in top notch products. We have partnerships with .... various African organizations especially African women agricultural groups. Help Africa by buying African products! Africa has fantastic products to offer the World.

Sheba Foods became a Wal-Mart vendor in March 2004, supplier number xxxxxxxxx, supplying products to the 24 Walmart store freezers, even though 29 was approved. Why? The answer lies in the perception of the managers on this minority product. African foods...hmm? One documented incident is briefly stated in a July 2005 letter to Mr. xxxxxxxxxx (please see attachment). Wal-Mart Global Diversity xxxxxxxxxxx. Both situations at the Gainesville Georgia Store Co-Manager and with Mr. , Wal-Mart Food Merchandiser, could have adverse effect on Wal-Mart if I go public with it. They were related in a letter to Mr. xxxxxxxxxx, Supplier Diversity xxxxxxxxxx in 2005. I did not ask him to act on it, I just wanted him aware of it. My goal is not to sue Wal-Mart, it is to be one of Wal-Mart's success stories. I need Wal-Mart to be one of my partners in offering African products thereby empowering the African continent. I have a dream of seeing African products have the same presence as Spanish foods in Wal-Mart and other stores. For this reason, I have tolerated comments and behaviors that were inappropriate. I am hoping that you can help make this dream happen. Wal-Mart would get such great positive press, which Wal-Mart really needs.

Over a month ago, I faxed a letter to Mr. Lee Scott stating many of the contents of this letter. I understand that he does not read all his mail, which could be the reason for the lack of response. As a Board Member, you are trusted to guide Wal-Mart in remaining a profitable company as well as contributing to better business practices. I am trusting you with the resolution this issue.

TO RECAP THE ISSUE:

1. MARCH 2005

    The Jollof Rice that was sold in the freezer was approved for 45 Wal-Mart Deli in (please see attachment).

2. MAY TO JULY 2005

    Despite numerous calls and letters to Wal-Mart. I was unsuccessful in getting a call back or response from Wal-Mart as to when to begin delivery of the Jollof Rice.

3. LATE JULY 2005

    Within 24 hours of calling Mr. Daft's office in Atlanta at Coca-Cola, Mr. Robert Newell, Wal-Mart House counsel calls me.

4. WALMART'S RESPONSE

Got a letter from Mr. Robert Newell, supporting the buyer's decision to not proceed with the rice.

5. SEPTEMBER 2005

I responded to Mr. Newell's letter. There was no rational basis for his response, since the rice is heated the same way as the Macaroni & Cheese and other items sold in hot deli. I asked numerous questions to help him see that there is no rational basis for Wal-Mart's position.

6. OCTOBER 2005

The buyer decided to proceed with 5 stores – a three month trial; 40 stores remaining.

7. LATE NOVEMBER 2005

a. Wal-Mart supplier department states that my Dun & Bradstreet's rating was a 9. They needed it to be under 7. I felt this was another of Wal-Mart's excuse to not move forward.

b. In calling Dun & Bradstreet, they *could and would not* disclose whom the negative information was coming from for me to correct it.

c. I told xxxxxxxxx, the buyer, that I know that the rating is a major mistake and that once it was cleared up, I need him to proceed with all 45 stores. Dun and Bradstreet *refused* to name the companies to call, not knowing who my accusers were was difficult.

d. I prayed and miraculously within a week, the rating came down to a 3. Halleluyah!

8. DECEMBER 2005

The information on the Jollof Rice has not been put in the system for the stores to order it. I missed out on the busy holiday season.

9. JANUARY – MARCH 2006

a. Store 1184 orders 4 boxes (16 bags) even though the product was not in their system. Many thanks to this store.

b. Store 1340 tells me they have no warmer and therefore can't try the rice. Replaced this store with Store 5390.

c. Store 1047 tells me that management told them to disregard the trial. Replaced this store with Store 3205.

d. Store 2154, kept postponing time for a decision. Last week, the co-manager xxxxxx told me to call in two weeks. She needed to confer with the new store manager who may or may not start in two weeks…hmm

e. Store 1578, still trying to catch up with xxxxxxxxx, the store co-manager for a decision. He was quite receptive to trying the product. I seem to miss him each time I called but left messages. Spoke three times with xxxxxxxxx, deli manager and she said to keep trying to get the decision from xxxxxxxxx.

10. FEBRUARY – MARCH 2006

Jollof Rice finally in system for two out of five stores. Store 3205 Lithia Springs and 5390 Marietta stores waiting to order but need the product in their system.

11. MARCH 2006

a. Spent over an hour on delivery in Store 1184 for product was not in the system and scale shows "item not found." Called Bentonville, and product was received by store. Scale input to be corrected later.

   b. Two weeks later, once scale worked, I noticed the retail
price at ___, cost to Wal-Mart is ___. This is a 203%
mark-up. *This product is priced to fail!* I emailed
___ ced Mr. ___ asking if this pricing was the standard
for the products in the Deli. I suggested ___. No
response from either as of today, March 28, 2006.

My REQUEST

1. **I need Wal-Mart to honor the letter approving the Jollof Rice 45 stores listed.** I went through
an intensive process to get the stores. I deserved a fair trial of the product. One argument could
be that it was tried in the freezer. It did not do as well giving where it was placed, etc. Some
stores had it on the top shelves at the end of the door, with no light on the top shelf. It is quite
frustrating to go through the approval process, then have to go back to managers who are
insensitive to the effort one has put forth.

2. **Place the orders for the rice and notify the Deli Managers of the new product.** I am sure that
is how is happened for the Macaroni and Cheese and other products sold in the hot deli. I
would follow-up by visiting the stores to clarify cooking instructions and confirm dates for food
sampling in the stores.

It would seems that Wal-Mart actively works to eliminate small business from its vendor list, while
presenting good front on doing business with minority suppliers. I am curious to see the number of
minorities supplying to Wal-Mart, what products are being supplied and how long they have been a
supplier. It would be interesting to get their experience with Wal-Mart. When I tell people that I am a
Wal-Mart vendor, they offer me their condolences instead of congratulations. This needs to change!

Wal-Mart has perfected being sued. Wal-Mart needs to perfect having wonderful vendor relationships.
If Wal-Mart continues with its current stance, it will hurt going into the African continent. Sheba Foods
is from Algeria to Zimbabwe and will become important to Wal-Mart if it decides to open store in the
African continent, especially Nigeria and West African countries.

SUGGESTIONS

While I have your attention, in 2005, Wal-Mart announced funds to help up to 9 small businesses. In
calling the company administering the fund, I found out the $4+ Million sales criteria. During a
business meeting, the concession was that this was another "look good" marketing scheme for Wal-
Mart who takes in the minority businesses through the front door, only to kick them out through the
back door.

In my opinion, the money would be better spent with greater goodwill if Wal-Mart would include
small/minority companies in their marketing. For example, use Sheba Foods for 2007 Black History
Month marketing. How effective has the past Black History Months' marketing been? How about a
section in each Wal-Mart department showcasing the small/minority products? How about a
small/minority business month? ___ where all these companies have displays and/or samples in the
store. How about a small/minority business focus group in each state to communicate with Wal-Mart
our experiences and suggestions of solutions? I would be glad to help put all these in place.

Please feel free to contact me at 770.962.1000 or cell xxxxxxxxx or email ___@shebafoods.com. I look
forward to hearing from you. Thanks for your attention.

Sincerely,
Kunmi Oluleye

(1) I wanted to walk them through the process of warming the rice; and

(2) Do a demo on the first day. Given it was five stores, I did not have to hire additional staff for demos.

Staff was needed when doing demos the same Saturday, in all five stores. I did two demos (two stores) in one day. On Saturdays, from eleven a.m. — three p.m., another from four p.m. — eight p.m. My staff did only one store per day. On Sundays, given that Georgia is the "Bible Belt," from two p.m. — six p.m. In the past, I had to do demos and deliveries because of distance. Now I did deliveries one day, rested the next and demos the third day. A much lighter schedule.

The buyer and I agreed that I would update him and his VP on a weekly basis via email. The update included the number of deliveries, demo schedule and any issues encountered at the stores. I gladly updated as requested.

DAY 1 OF DELI JOLLOF RICE

The deli staff had other logistics to address prior to opening at ten a.m. I didn't want to interfere with their tasks. I generally started my deli sales setup after ten a.m. I told the managers to remove at least two bags of rice from the freezer the previous day and place it in the refrigerator, so that it would have thawed the next morning. For those who remembered, the rice had thawed but still cold. We put the bag in the steamer for about 40 minutes. Poured it into the pan it would be sold in. For those who forgot, I put the bag in the microwave to thaw. Emptied the bag into a container and microwaved. Once hot, poured into the steam tray it would be sold in.

While the deli staff were attending to their logistics prior opening, I was busy setting up my demo table, so passer bys saw there was food to be sampled later. I then taped signs on the Wal-Mart entry doors. Once the deli rice was ready for sale, I handed out flyers throughout the store, telling people the demo was about to start. By the time I got back to the demo table, there would be people waiting to taste the rice. As people went by, I invited them to the table by saying: "Please join me for a taste of exotic African cuisine." Their eyebrows would go up, they stopped and took a sample.

WHAT HAPPENED BETWEEN MAY TO JULY 2006?

The Wal-Mart's Hot Deli policy states that to guarantee freshness, the warmed up food must be thrown out every two hours if not sold. I have bought chicken and other products in the hot deli, prior to, during and after my Jollof Rice was sold. The food is not always thrown out after two hours. I have returned hot deli products to customer service because the chicken, potato wedges was quite stiff—dried out. The shelf life on the Jollof Rice is 18 hours, which means that it can be warmed, left out on the counter and still be safe to eat 18 hours after. Really? Yes, really. Africans are master preservative specialists. The all natural seasonings prevent bacteria breakdown, yet maintaining its tastiness. Jollof Rice made the previous day actually tastes better the next day, because the seasonings and rice have merged better.

The demo table was always a few yards from the hot deli case. It made it easy to direct people who wanted to purchase the product after tasting it.   We saw people buy half to two pounds of rice. The rice became so popular that two managers decided to offer it as one of the side items for the Wal-Mart chicken platter. One manager went through 23 bags in one week. The rice was a hit, a disappointment to Wal-Mart. Then the stores began to take delivery and not put the rice out. Most of the time when I visited the stores, the rice was no where in sight. I checked my delivery sheet to view the last delivery and quantity, asked the sales associate if they ran out. They had a few cases in the freezer. The sales associates told me they were instructed to make the rice available for sale only when I did demos. I would have to do demos everyday, all day in all five stores. That was absurd! No one from Bentonville communicated that to me.

To make things worse, products were damaged out. Wal-Mart claimed it did not sell. They couldn't claim it expired for the date stamp showed one year. The general rule is that frozen products have a two-year shelf life. I certainly don't expect the rice to be on hand for any more than two months.   One of the Wal-Mart receivers said to me: "I check your product in, I work five days a week, eat from that deli everyday and not once have I seen your product in the hot case. Where are they putting it?" That was the situation in all the stores. What am I to do now?

SECRET SHOPPERS

I enlisted a number of people who lived or worked near one of the five Wal-Mart Stores. Two of them were Pastors with African congregations. Their churches were within five minutes of two of the Wal-Mart stores. They told me that they announced the Jollof Rice availability in the deli to their congregation, but the members couldn't find it each time they went to any of the stores. My Pastor friends decided to make the trips themselves, and confirmed it was not put out. The sales associates confirmed to them that the Jollof Rice was in stock, they just didn't put it out that day. Other friends would go in on various days and times to all the stores. A few saw it on certain days, but most of the time the Jollof Rice was not available for sale. Even though I communicated this problem via email several times to the buyer and VP, the situation got worse. The stores began reporting high wastage from the Jollof Rice they supposedly warmed up for sale. How can there be wastage on rice kept in the freezer?

TREACHERY IN THE DELI CAMP

Three of the stores had African deli associates. I asked them to tell me if the products truly was not selling. All stated that the Wal-Mart customers loved the Jollof Rice. The managers had been instructed by Bentonville to do all they could to show poor sales. This instructions were passed to the associates. All three stores had the same story. I doubt they spoke with each other prior to my conversing with them.

"What is the issue?" A question I posed to one manager who admired my determination to survive within Wal-Mart. The manager confirmed that the mandate was true. I pleaded for a copy of the email. Once I confirmed that the rice was not the issue. I had to conceal the manager's identity, but had to have it documented that I knew the sabotage instruction existed. My weekly report to the buyer and VP confirmed that their instructions were executed. I picked a store who had a manager that I knew did not like me. This manager was an African-American woman. I told her that I wanted to have a discussion as to why my products were being damaged out for no reason. She made appointments for our conversation. I confirmed the appointment with her a day prior. When I got there, she was either on vacation, in a meeting, just left for lunch or other excuses. Two hours wasted each time driving back and forth. We never had a conversation.

I eventually had the conversation with the manager she reported to. Her supervisor was shocked when I told him my feedback came from the sales associates. His response was that for starters, the deli manager who avoided me spoke highly of the Jollof Rice because it was selling. He shared that sales associates didn't like her. There was rivalry between them, which of course, he was attending to. I forwarded an email to Bentonville in my weekly report, documenting all that is stated here. Got no response.

No newspaper or television wanted to run the Wal-Mart story for fear of repercussion. My options were running out. Time to reach out to my African-American leaders, hopefully they can help. I called Congresswoman Cynthia McKinney. Sent the same letter to Ambassador Andrew Young, Ambassador Carl Masters, both men of Goodworks International, LLC (GWI Consulting) and Mr. Jesse Jackson. For many weeks, after I had sent the letters to the men, I called their offices and got no response.

AMBASSADORS YOUNG & MASTERS

Why write to Ambassadors Young and Masters? At the time I sent the letter, Ambassador Young served as consultant to Wal-Mart. I heard from a reputable source that during Wal-Mart's relationship with Ambassador Young, he got approval for Wal-Mart to build in Nigeria. I have not been able to verify the information from either Wal-Mart or Ambassador Young's office. Ambassadors Young and Masters were and still are consultants to Nigeria. I was naive to think that they might help this African in need. I thought their assistance would enhance their image with African countries. Ambassador Masters' tie to Nigeria is very close. His elaborate wedding ceremony to Hope Masters of the Sullivan Foundation, was held in Abuja, Nigeria. I can only speculate that the Nigerian government contributed handsomely to the event.

In May 2006, I complained to a man I recently met, about the lack of response from Ambassador Young's office. I had no clue the man had a relationship with Ambassador Young. I was shocked when he called Ambassador Young's cell phone right in front of me, and Ambassador Young answered. The man related my issue and desire for a meeting. Ambassador Young stated that he had not read the letter I sent him. Within 24 hours, I got lip service from the Goodworks' woman assigned to the Goodworks-Wal-Mart relationship. Many weeks later, after numerous emails and phone calls (left messages) to follow-up with the woman, she called to inform me that Wal-Mart said the problem had been fixed. I told her the problem still existed. For example, Lithonia had reported to me that they sold 23 bags within one week, which was expected. Later the store reported they were not selling at all and need to discontinue

April 25, 2006

Dear Ambassador Young:

I would like to request a meeting with you to discuss my issue with Wal-Mart with the hope that we are able to find a solution. I've tried numerous times to get an appointment since I heard he was working with Wal-Mart. I need your help  to keep Wal-Mart from dismissing a product, which helps bridge the gap between Africans and African Americans, as well as, has high potential in sales. I am Kunmi Oluleye, President of Sheba Foods, the First and Only Manufacturer of Fresh Frozen African Cuisine. I have survived being in Wal-Mart for over two years with the Grace of God. Sheba Foods is a certified Women Business Enterprise (WBE) and Minority Business Enterprise (MBE) company based in Georgia.

African cuisine is one of the tastiest and healthy foods one can eat and I need to get Americans, especially African-Americans into experiencing it. I believe they'll love it. It will be the beginning of loving Africa. Africans are ready to welcome home our brothers and sisters. I want to help with the journey home by introducing them to the tastes of Africa.

Please see the attached letters to Wal-Mart which summarizes my struggles. God gave me the wisdom to write and send the April letter to all the Wal-Mart board of directors. It was quite a task getting all their contact information. I'll go down in Wal-Mart's history as a person who won a fight without going to court. Thank you Jesus! This pressure on Wal-Mart got them to have the Jollof Rice debuted in the five stores about two weeks ago. One store started with 5 cases (20 bags), sold out and ordered 2 more cases (8 bags) a week later. To date 34 cases has been delivered altogether to the five stores (136 bags = 680 lbs of rice). The general comment from ALL the managers is that the rice is selling and people want it with the chicken sold in the hot steam trays.

In the beginning, the stores were not putting the rice out everyday and only put it out when they knew that I was doing a food demo. I communicated the customer requests and rice not put out to the buyer. Then on April 20th, I had a conversation with one of the stores and the deli manager told me that they wasted 23 bags of rice it was not sold. I was stunned. He told me that the rice was not selling. This was not true because I spent hours in that store doing a food demo and watched people buy it in the deli. I watched the deli sell 2 bags (10lbs) within two hours. I then asked what quantity the store sold and he said 2 bags, which I bought when I did the demo. I told him that I don't buy the products used in demos, I bring them in. He was silence for he knew I catch him in a lie.

This past weekend, on April 22nd, CNN Inside Africa aired a story on Sheba Foods (taped in February 2006), which should increase awareness of my products. How many minorities are doing business with Wal-Mart if few, why? I know a few reasons why. How does one get in? What is the retention rate of small/minority business? What is Wal-Mart doing to change the numbers? Please visit our website for more information on Sheba Foods, www.shebafoods.com/news.aspx has more media exposure details.

I can be reached by _____@shebafoods.com, cell _____, office 770.982.1000
          I look forward to hearing from you soon.

Sincerely,
Kunmi Oluleye

the trial before the 90 days was over.

The Goodworks' woman stated that there is nothing Ambassador Young could do about the situation. She continued that was not his department. What if it was his daughter or sister having this issue with Wal-Mart? One would think given the relationship Ambassador Young has with Nigeria, he and his office would be responsive to a Nigerian in need, especially since the issue involved another one of his clients, Wal-Mart. Since weeks had passed, I asked if Ambassador Young had read my letter. I hoped to hear from him directly. The Goodworks' woman stated that did he read it, but unfortunately was traveling for the next few months, making a meeting not possible. I knew she was lying. I shared that Ambassador Young has no credibility with Nigerians, adding that I am not sure which Africans he has credibility with, given the responses from his office. I told her that it seemed to me that like others, he and/or his office are pimping Africa.

What exactly has he done for Nigeria? Has Goodworks done anything for any African country without being overpaid for it? Goodworks could help change the bad perception created by the "419" or fraudulent image. Goodworks has done nothing to improve Nigeria's image. Yet, I read about multi-million dollar projects awarded to Goodworks. Ambassador Young does not show up at most Nigerian events in the U.S. unless paid for it. Many Nigerians hiss when you mention his name. The conversation between me and this Goodworks' woman got really heated. I was surprised she did not hang up. She gave me time to communicate my feelings. I extended her the same courtesy. She of course gave me a piece of her mind about Nigerians. At the end, I told her I would write a book about my Goodworks experience. She said: "Thank God we are in the U.S., where there is freedom of speech. It is a free country, you do whatever you need to do." The conversation ended on that note. Three or so days later, Ambassador Young made the statement that severed his relationship with Wal-Mart. To me justice was done, even though God's reprimanding of the Goodworks' woman came through Ambassador Young.

To be fair to Ambassador Young whom I have met and spoken with briefly a number of times. He is an absolutely sweet man with a good heart. His staff however give him a horrible image by what they do. Unfortunately, leaders are held responsible for the actions of their subordinates. I never spoke with him at any point in time on the Wal-Mart issue. He was aware given the phone call placed in my presence to his cell phone.

Note to Ambassador Young: It is time to retire, rest and grow old gracefully so your staff quits messing up your good name.

Mr. Jesse Jackson (also known as Reverend Jesse Jackson)

I feel the title Mr. is more appropriate for Jesse Jackson than Reverend, given he dropped out seminary and did not achieve any of the steps required for his title. If any of what I've read is true, the use of the title Reverend is "419." Even if he met the requirements, Mr. Jackson's behavior screams worse than an unbeliever, destroying the Reverend title. I am told that one of the Wal-Mart attorneys that I spoke with, about my Wal-Mart plight was one of Mr. Jackson's "boys". Even though his boy was great to speak with, listened with such care and promised to look into the issue. He later told me that Supplier Diversity and the Wal-Mart executives were handling it. In July 2007, my internet search results on Mr. Jackson were alarming.

I was overwhelmed with Kenneth Timmerman's compelling book, *"Shakedown: Exposing the Real Jesse Jackson."* My heart skipped beats for minutes. I highly recommend everyone, especially African Presidents to read this book. It is mind bugling. The West African journalist Tom Kamara, in assessing Jesse Jackson's record wrote that "Jackson is considered a civil rights leader in America, but in Africa he is a killers' rights leader." One website reported that Mr. Jackson argued against sanctions to defend the murderous Nigerian President Abacha's execution of a playwright and several other dissidents. Mr. Jackson's son Jonathan later received a Nigerian oil contract. With the title Reverend, he does not even appear to serve God on this side of Heaven. It seemed that Jesse Jackson vacations in Hell or maybe Hell is his headquarters. How does Mr. Jackson sleep at night?

I am generally fearless. I have never been scared of Wal-Mart or Ambassador Young, but I got really scared of mentioning Jesse Jackson in this book given the murders associated with him. Now I understand why people fear Wal-Mart. Affiliations with the likes Jesse Jackson keeps people in check. People who knew him personally back to the days of Martin Luther King, Jr., told me that Jesse Jackson is worse than Wal-Mart and would probably use my situation to get more favors from Wal-Mart. Hopefully, not at the price of my disappearance. His record makes Wal-Mart look like a saint. For those who don't believe his record is that bad, please read Kenneth Timmerman's book *"Shakedown: Exposing the Real Jesse Jackson."*

Note to Mr. Jackson: It's time to do right by your people —
African-Americans and Africans.

CONGRESSWOMAN CYNTHIA MCKINNEY

I am not political. I relate to people on how they
affect my life. I don't understand why so many people
dislike Congresswoman Cynthia McKinney. During my
Wal-Mart ordeal, she was my light in the dark. When I
called her office with my Wal-Mart issue, I was as much a
stranger to her as I was to Mr. Daft of Coca-Cola. Within
days she took time to listen and act on my behalf.
Congresswoman McKinney sent a letter to Wal-Mart
questioning the rational for all they've done with my Jollof
Rice in the deli. When I was invited by Wal-Mart's top
management to Bentonville to address my concerns,
Congresswoman McKinney was willing to accompany me.
After all, she is an attorney and I really needed her strength
and wisdom. She never asked for compensation. It was as
simple as Kunmi needs my help, let me see what I can do.
At that time she stayed in Washington, D.C., occasionally
in Atlanta.

In 2006, over 200 people unsubscribed from my
newsletter just because I included a section in the e-blast
thanking her for her help with the Wal-Mart issue. I would
be a total hypocrite to not include her in relating the Wal-
Mart experience. Some people would argue that the
association with Congresswoman McKinney contributed to
the Wal-Mart's outcome, I respectfully disagree. It think it
was the contrary. Her involvement got Wal-Mart to extend
me an invitation to Bentonville. Wal-Mart did not make
their decision to end the Jollof Rice trial, until it was clear

Congresswoman McKinney lost the election. I found her to be truthful and real. I know a lot of people loved me until this point. They are now ready to burn the book. You've paid for the book, please finish reading it.

Congresswoman McKinney showed up at many Nigerian events when invited, bestowed with numerous awards and recognition by various Nigerians organizations in the U.S. This is one person I would like the Nigerian government to hire as a consultant. She has a heart for Africa, especially African women. Anytime I saw her, with a big smile on her face, she'll say to me "here comes my Nigerian sister." She did not know about my writing this book and will discover my comments about her when she reads it, same as the others. To me, her record shows she stands and fights for justice. I love her spirit. For curiosity sake, prior to the election, I called her Congressional replacement to see if he would help with the Wal-Mart issue. He never responded.

Note to Congresswoman Cynthia McKinney: Thank you so very much from the bottom of my heart! I appreciate your holding my hands when others refused to. I hope the Almighty God sends help to you at your time of need, in Jesus Name.

JOLLOF TRIAL OVER

I was alone at the plant where my products were processed when the call came to my cell phone. There was no cooking at the time and it suddenly got stuffy in the plant. I had to go outside. It was the Wal-Mart VP that I've been conversing with over the last few months.

July 24, 2006

WalMart Senior Management
Wal-Mart Stores
702 S.W. 8th Street
Bentonville, AR 72716

Dear Mr. XXXXXXX :

Congresswoman McKinney will not be available until sometime in August 2006 giving how the elections turned out, and the runoff slated for August 2006. Is the trial over for the 5 stores? In waiting for her assistance, I decided to get Wal-Mart's position on the rice trial, ask for trial in remaining 40 stores.

There was sabotage of the Jollof Rice in the deli during the trial. I have evidence that the managers were instructed to put up with me for 90 days, giving the letter I wrote to the board of directors. They were to do whatever it took to show the Jollof Rice with poor sales. Since my products debuted in Wal-Mart in 2004, I have actively worked to give Wal-Mart positive publicity. In 2004, I initiated a study on Wal-Mart's success on the African continent. Ambassador Young can help Wal-Mart put up structures and stock the shelves in any African country, Sheba Foods becomes important thereafter. Since Ambassador Young is on Wal-Mart's payroll, I decided to have Congresswoman McKinney assist me.

Many people are waiting to see the resolution of the current issue. The Jollof Rice is one of my best products and I will not allow Wal-Mart to label it otherwise. It did not do as well as it should have because your personnel sabotaged it.

The newsletter that you brought to my attention generated 15 U.S. companies who had experience with Wal-Mart, 3 of those did not do business with Wal-Mart, but had interesting stories to tell. I shared one of them with   , your diversity person, who confirmed the woman relating the story in Miami. Numerous others and organizations asked how they can be of help. Let's not make this an issue of Goliath (Wal-Mart) vs. David (Sheba Foods). Wal-Mart should be concerned about losing Sheba Foods as a supplier. I'll like to continue the trial, this time with all 45 stores.

Thank you for your attention. Please feel free to contact me at 770.982.1000 or email. I look forward to hearing from you soon.

Sincerely,
Kunmi Oluleye

Mr. VP: Ms. Oluleye, it's _ _ _ _ _ from Wal-Mart. How are you?

Kunmi: Good thank you.

Mr. VP: I wanted to let you know that we won't be continuing with the trial.

Kunmi: No surprise there.

Mr. VP: We gave it a good try. Your products got more attention than most.

Kunmi: I respectful disagree. I feel the product was sabotaged and will fight you and Wal-Mart hard.

Mr. VP: I wish you well Ms. Oluleye. Have a good day.

Kunmi: Thank you and you have a good day as well.

Even though I knew the trial was over before I heard the words, I subconsciously wished I was wrong. When the conversation started, I knew I must remember it, for it was one of the defining moments of my life. As we were talking, I was walking to my car. I wanted to be sitting in a comfortable private space. I had reached the back of my car when we said goodbye. I took a deep breath, exhaled, put the cell phone on the trunk, stopped and looked around. No tears.

The sky was clear, blue, with the sun shining so brightly. Even though it was hot, it wasn't humid. A wonderful peaceful breeze that started blowing when I stepped out of the plant was still blowing. It was an absolutely beautiful day! I look up and out came the words: "Holy Jesus, I have lost!" The flood of tears began and were unstoppable. I placed my head on the trunk of my car and sobbed uncontrollably. For hours, in between the sobs I recounted the past months' events. The tears were mixed. Happy that the struggle was over, no more reports of perfectly good products being damaged. No more wasting of resources doing demos only for Wal-Mart to not put the products out. Sad that Wal-Mart won again. I could hear my husband saying "see all the money you wasted continuing with Wal-Mart when that could have gone to pay the house bills, and all that time.......etc." I wasn't sure which hurt more. So much pain! I would have gladly stayed with Wal-Mart, and taken more beating till death, like a battered woman.

I had my pity party that day. I was super worn out with the crying. Sat in my car, all windows rolled down, laid the seat flat as far back as it would go. I had cried so much that even when I remembered a bad moment that I had not cried about earlier there were no tears. As I stared at the sky, my favorite Psalm 121 in Yoruba quietly creeped into my spirit. It seemed to be on replay. Reciting it in my mind, I drifted off to sleep to be awaken by my children's call wondering where I was. It had gotten dark. I had slept for at least four hours. I got out of the car, locked up the plant and embarked on the 1.5 hours drive home.

Should I tell my husband? That was the question. I did not tell my husband for many weeks. The tears still came for a while when I told those I considered friends.

Beaten but Not Broken!

YORUBA   PSALM 121   ENGLISH

1 Emi o gbè oju si oke mi si oke wonni, Nibo ni iranlowo mi ti nwa?

1 I lift up my eyes to the hills, where does my help come from?

2 Iranlowo mi ti owo Oluwá wá, ti o da Orun on aiye.

2 My help comes from the LORD, the Maker of Heaven and Earth.

3 On ki yio jê ki êsê mi kio yê; êniti npa mi mo ki yio tõgbe.

3 He will not let my foot slip— He who watches over me does not slumber;

4 Kiyesi i, eniti npa Israeli mo, ki itõgbe, bëni ki isùn.

4 Indeed, He who watches over Israel neither slumbers nor sleeps.

5 Oluwa li olupanmo mi, Oluwa li ojiji mi li owo Otún mi.

5 The LORD watches over me the LORD is my shade at my right hand;

6 Orùn ki yio pa mi nigba osan, tabi osupa nigba oru.

6 The sun will not harm me by day, nor the moon by night.

7 Oluwa yio pa mi mo kuro ninu ibi gbogbo; yio pa okàn mi mo.

7 The LORD keeps me from all harm—
he watches over my life;

8 Oluwa yio pa àlo at àbo mi mo lati igba yi lo, ati titi lailai.

8 The LORD watches my over my comings and goings both now and forevermore.

Chapter Six

Wal-Mart Germany Exit & African Entry

There are two types of people besides relatives
who can ask you for money — they pay no interest
on the money nor ever pay it back.
Who you ask? - Pastors and Robbers!
Kermit Simms

I got a call in August 2006, the friend on the other line was ecstatic: "Kunmi, Kunmi, have you heard!?" Heard what!? I responded. "Kunmi, Wal-Mart got kicked out of Germany, lost millions or billions am not sure which, in any case they are no longer in Germany. It is all over the news!!!" "Really?" I responded, serves them right for what they did to me and all atrocities they continue to commit here. My friend continues: "They think they can go into a foreign country and continue their bad behavior. Thank you Germany for showing Wal-Mart the door!!! Imagine that, months ago them and Ambassador Young parted, now its goodbye to Germany, whose next? China or India?"

Then we began speculating. What happens when Wal-Mart sets up shop in Nigeria, and it's time to exit like Germany? A cartoon suddenly flashed in my mind where Wal-Mart executives are running, papers flying in the air. According to the African culture, a woman with a broom is sweeping behind their feet to fade-out their steps. "Run Wal-Mart, Run!" was the caption. We both had a great laugh that day. My friend's call came shortly after the Wal-Mart VP's conversation ending the Jollof Rice trial. My guess is that the VP thought I would sue Wal-Mart in my comment that I'll fight back hard. I knew I would fight them where I could win—by writing this book. Yes, I have already won! How can Wal-Mart do right in Africa, when they did not do right by me?

I didn't research the story about Wal-Mart's Germany exit at the time. I took my friend's word for it. I decided to get the complete story when I began writing this Chapter. To my great disappointment, Wal-Mart didn't get kicked out as I thought. Wal-Mart kicked themselves out of Germany taking a billion dollar loss. Whether they were kicked out or they left on their own terms, $1 billion was lost. To me, justice was served.

The rest of this Chapter shares my view about Wal-Mart's Germany exit and likelihood of occurrences should they embark on an African entry. I share similarities between Germans and Africans. In digesting information about Wal-Mart international operations, Wal-Mart tries to adapt the community it enters to its U.S. ways of operation. They should be adapting their business practices to the countries they enter. Wal-Mart currently operates in: Argentina, Brazil, Canada, China, Costa Rica, El Salvador, Guatemala, Honduras, Japan, Mexico, Nicaragua, Puerto Rico and the United Kingdom.

WAL-MART LEAVES GERMANY

The giant retailer clearly did not do its homework prior to its entry into the German market. John Davison, Managing VP at Gartner states that "retailers seeking to grow internationally should recognize that retail formats, systems and processes designed to provide economies of scale in home markets don't always translate to different countries." Wal-Mart's retreat, abandoning its stores and merchandise represents the second time in 2006 that it has bailed out of a foreign country. In May 2006, Wal-Mart announced it would sell its 16 stores in South Korea. The Germany exit represented Wal-Mart's most significant foreign retrenchment since it began expanding its stores internationally in the early 1990s.

After eight years of trying in Germany, Wal-Mart said it couldn't turn around its 85 German stores, which had lost money. Wal-Mart Chief Executive Lee Scott stated that the stores it purchased in Germany "....were difficult stores. It was clearly a very challenging market for us, that we have not figured out." Admitting defeat, the world's largest retailer sold its German operations to rival German retailer Metro AG, giving up its foothold in continental Europe, at a time when it was trying to rejuvenate growth through international expansion. Wal-Mart's U.S. low prices were not low enough for the German shoppers who are frugal and demanding. Will Wal-Mart's entry into

Africa, its slogan of low price guarantee, be low enough for the poor African? I don't think so. The poor African whose wages are quite low, will continue to perceive supermarkets a luxury place to shop.

POOR MARKET ENTRY STRATEGY

I am surprised that the market research Wal-Mart did prior to Germany's entry, did not show the issues that caused its exit. Here are a few of the issues:

A. German shoppers are frugal and demanding.

B. German shoppers are accustomed to buying merchandise strictly based on price. They are willing to buy laundry detergent at one store and then go to another to get a better price on paper towels. That behavior is called "basket splitting." It is the antithesis of what American shoppers like: one-stop shopping. Wal-Mart's strategy in the U.S. and elsewhere is its one stop shopping. Offering a wide array of goods.

C. German shoppers who were used to bagging their own purchases, were turned off by this American practice.

D. German employees objected to American style workplace rules such as Wal-Mart's prohibition of romantic relationships between supervisors and employees. A lawsuit by the German workers forced Wal-Mart to lift its ban.

E. There were regulations restricting store hours and other retailing basics. Germany's stringent operating laws required it to close stores by six p.m. on weekdays and four p.m. on Saturdays, although those restrictions eased a bit in recent years.

F. No loss leaders. It is a retail trick to lure shoppers into the stores by selling goods below cost. The retailer knows that those shoppers will buy other goods, thereby making up on the goods they took a loss on. This retail practice is against the law in Germany. Did Wal-Mart think they could bribe their way into changing laws in Germany? If yes, there were wrong.

I found the Germany failure interesting. The issues encountered are sure to repeat themselves in certain Africa countries if Wal-Mart uses the same entry strategy. How would the African landscape change with the presence of this retail giant? In answering this question, let's look at the function of the african marketplace.

FUNCTION OF THE TRADITIONAL AFRICAN MARKETPLACE

African shoppers are also frugal and demanding. Many of the food retail outlets in the African countries are through hawkers, mini-convenient stores at gas stations, small stands or stands in a formalize marketplace setting. In February 2007, while in Nairobi, Kenya, I had a chance to visit the Village Market. There were numerous shops including a supermarket called Nakumatt. I was quite impressed with the Nakumatt layout, product offerings, pricing and staffing. They understood the African marketplace and survival. On certain days at the Village Market, there is a Masai market, which brings local suppliers to sell their goods. One of the reasons I go "home" is because I miss the bargaining aspect of the marketplace. Anywhere on the African continent is "home" for me. At Nakumatt, I found that the price was low enough that I didn't miss out on the haggling.

I worried that supermarkets such as Wal-Mart will destroy the traditional African marketplace by taking its customers. I remember going to the market with my Mother. It took hours to go a very short distance. Why? The market women offer more than goods to their customers, they are their therapists, doctors, friends, match-makers and creditors. The young women share their personal, family or marital issues with the market women. It would be hard to incorporate that function into a supermarket setting. Because supermarkets will not be able to incorporate the traditional marketplace function into their settings, the traditional African marketplace should survive.

AFRICAN SUPERMARKETS TRANSFORMING THE FOOD RETAIL SECTOR

From an economic standpoint, the growth of African supermarkets should help reduce poverty. Potential benefits include: modern buildings, creation of employment and implementation of state-of-the art computer systems. There is no doubt that Wal-Mart's infrastructure, procurement system and other efficiencies will benefit Africa. From my research, I concluded that the African supermarkets has three target markets.

1. Tourists. I would think that tourists would prefer to shop in an African supermarket, than the Traditional

African Marketplace because of convenience, and fear of venturing into unfamiliar surroundings.

2. The returning Africans. Many Africans are relocating back to their countries. It is natural to desire the conveniences enjoyed abroad. This is probably one of the factors contributing to the middle class growth, and rapid rise of supermarkets in Egypt, Kenya, Ghana, Nigeria and South Africa.

3. Middle class natives. As African countries become stable, financial stability raises the income of the Africans. Supermarkets offer them the opportunity to enjoy foreign products without leaving their country. The truth is that if most Africans residing abroad could earn the same income at home, as they do abroad, they would move back to their country. Current foreign investments and initiatives in African countries is making the relocations and increase in wages a reality for many Africans.

The existence of supermarkets had brought order and cleanliness to many African cities. In a few places, it greatly reduced the numbers of street hawkers. I wondered if those street hawkers became supermarket employees, given the employment opportunity the supermarkets required. One of the things that I liked about Nakumatt, was that many of the products on their shelves and freezer, were either locally made in Kenya or from other African countries. For supermarkets to reduce poverty, not only do they have to provide employment, support the local farmers, but also be an outlet for African entrepreneurs.

Supermarkets present excellent income opportunities for local suppliers and farmers. For years, African farms have supplied products to Europe, America and other foreign markets. Supplying commodities such as spices, cocoa, tea leaves, coffee beans and Shea Butter. The farmers will now have an additional outlet to market their products.

COMMONALITIES BETWEEN GERMAN AND AFRICAN PRACTICES

One of the problems that Wal-Mart had in Germany was violation of cultural practices, two of which were:

1. *Wal-Mart's prohibition for their employees to accept gifts and inducements.* A common German practice. Africans are about gifts, either cash, product or in kind. Its our way of life and has been from the beginning of time. If I invite you to my house for dinner, the dinner is a gift. Come hungry, eat a lot and take some home. I feel the Wal-Mart rule is somewhat hypocritical. What about the slotting fees U.S. supermarkets charge? To me, slotting fees are bribery or corporate gifts. A slotting fee is what suppliers pay supermarkets for better shelf space, or to keep the competition out. The amount is not recorded in financial statements and is perfectly legal in the U.S. According to Wikipedia, the amount per product ranges from $25,000 to $250,000. My guess would be that this is paid yearly.

    Wikipedia continued: "In addition to slotting fees, retailers may also charge promotional, advertising and stocking fees. According to an FTC study, the practice is "widespread" in the supermarket industry. Many grocers earn more profit from agreeing to carry a manufacturer's product than they do from actually selling the product to retail consumers. According to retailers, fees serve to efficiently allocate scarce retail shelf space, help balance the risk of new product failure between manufacturers and retailers, and serve to widen retail distribution for manufacturers by mitigating retail competition."

My explanation. Slotting fees are "required" gifts. If you pay me between $25,000 to $250,000, you can put your product here. That does not include other expenses the supplier needs to incur to make sure the product sells. It is more profitable for Wal-Mart and other supermarkets to stock large corporations' products, than minority products. Ingles and Wal-Mart did not charge Sheba Foods slotting fees.

2. *Wal-Mart's prohibition of romantic relationships between co-workers if one is in a position of influence—supervisor and subordinate.* A common practice in the German and African workplace. Sexual harassment is not a crime on the African continent. Men can still marry as many wives as they want. Married men have as many girlfriends as they can handle. The African wife looks the other way, pretending she does not know. Corporate resources will be used to entertain those relationships. The foreign company that does not factor this into the market entry strategy is sure to fail, as Wal-Mart did in Germany. I am definitely not supportive of infidelity, nor condone this unfair treatment of women, but it is the African reality.

I could not stop laughing reading this May 27, 2007, *Wall Street Journal*, article posted on workinglife.org. If this had happened in Africa or Germany, given love affairs are entertained in the workplace, there would be no need for termination or lawsuit. They'll both get a slap on the wrist, asked to kiss and make-up and it is back to business as usual. I call the article *As The Wal-Mart World Turns* — a love affair, claims of corporate gifts (bribery) and so on.

The article reads:

Fired Wal-Mart Stores marketing executive Julie Roehm took aim at the retailer's chief executive and other senior executives, claiming they skirted its ethics policy, accepting travel, concert tickets and preferential prices on yachts and jewelry. Ms. Roehm contends that Chief Executive H. Lee Scott and his family have close ties to financier Irwin Jacobs, whose companies provide services and products to Wal-Mart, according to her filing in U.S. District Court, Detroit. She alleged their ties go "beyond a business relationship" that Wal-Mart's ethics policies dictate. Mr. Jacobs, reached today, denied any favoritism.

The court filing is the latest twist in a war of words between the high-profile advertising executive and the world's largest retailer. In March, Bentonville, Ark.-based Wal-Mart described what it said were suggestive personal emails and cited unnamed co-workers describing an admission of an affair between Ms. Roehm and a subordinate, former Vice President Sean Womack. You kind of figured this one would get ugly.

Wal-Mart later released copies of the Ms.

Roehm's love letters to the court.

WHICH COMPANIES WILL DO RIGHT BY AFRICA?

My two picks are Costco and Ahold. That is not to say that these are the only two companies with great ethics. My interactions with these two companies showed the quality of their leadership, embracing diversity, respect for their suppliers, employees and concern for the environments they function in. I am encouraged that their business practices will respect Africa, its people, resources and culture. They will not only do well in Africa, they will do right by Africa.

COSTCO

Costco and Sam's Club (Wal-Mart) sell similar products. However, Costco pays higher wages and has excellent benefits for its employees than Wal-Mart. The compensation package Costco offers attracts and keeps higher-skilled workers, which in turn, better sells its products. Costco's affluent shoppers, whose income averages $74,000, will appreciate the quality products that Africa has to offer.

AHOLD

Ahold operates in the U.S. through Stop & Shop, Giant Stores and US Foodservice. Not so long ago, I wrote to the President of Ahold, Anders Moberg, desiring to supply African products to their stores. I was pleased to get an email stating that he would like that as well. Later, Sheba

Foods was invited to exhibit at the 2006 US Foodservice Food Show in Atlanta, giving me a complimentary booth space valued at $5,000. It was wonderful exposure. Sheba Foods products were approved for Stop & Shop and available through US Foodservice.

Prior to exhibiting at the U.S. Foodservice show, Ahold's African personnel in South Africa and Ghana, helped in identifying potential food suppliers for Sheba Foods. The Stop & Shop Supplier Diversity Director is one of the rarest of Director's that I've come across. Generally, most Supplier Diversity departments are ineffective. He not only sent me information, but followed up on how things were progressing. When I needed help selecting stores to begin trials in, unlike the Wal-Mart buyer, he educated me in the selection process.

I look forward to seeing Costco and Ahold stores in Africa!

Chapter Seven

Who is buying African food in U.S. Supermarkets?

---

*Change your network and
you'll change your net worth.*
HOTEP

The major supermarkets that I am referring to are the likes of Wal-Mart and Stop & Shop. The African foods in discussion are those of the Sub-sahara's African countries. South African products, especially wines, are well known and accepted because South Africa was settled by the Dutch. Its product labels and packaging mimics that of Europe which is complete with Nutrition Facts, ingredient list and other pertinent information. The North Africans (Morocco to Egypt) don't think they are Africans because of their complexion which is closer to the Arabs. Given Morrocco to Egypt is on the African continent, they are Africans. Their cuisine is considered Mediterranean, with product packaging also similar to that of Europe.

Sub-sahara's African countries have recognized that there is market for their African foods in the U.S. and Europe. To make their products acceptable and competitive, the suppliers in the sub-sahara's African countries are putting labels on their products, to be inline with the rest of the world. Nigeria now has a government body called the National Agency for Food and Drug Administration (NAFDAC) which ensures the quality and appropriate labeling of food products for import or export.

The sub-saharan African suppliers must invest in better packaging and labels, as well as, do more marketing. Africa is full of herbs and roots that could put penicillin to shame, but until studies prove me right and products packaged with acceptable labels, we stay with penicillin.

Who is buying African foods in major supermarkets? White people—Caucasians. Surprise! This next question should not be a surprise. Who invests in high-end African Art? Caucasians. So naturally, food follows. Sheba Foods target market is mainstream America, hoping to be the food and cultural bridge to Africa. The demographics shown below are results from my demos and catering events done over the years.

70% Caucasians

20% Africans

8% other ethnic groups

2% African-Americans

YOU EAT AFRICAN FOOD EVERYDAY

African food is not as foreign as people think. Majority of U.S. Southern cuisine and Soul Food originated from Africa. Similar ingredients, just prepared differently. Okra originated in Ethiopia, which at some point in time included Eritrea. It traveled to Egypt, then Sudan, then India before arriving in the U.S., specifically Louisiana, to be called Gumbo. According to Wikipedia: The name "okra" is of West African origin and is cognate with "ọ̀kụ̀rụ̀" in Igbo, a Nigerian language and tribe. In various Bantu languages, okra is called "kingombo". Find out which African countries speak the Bantu language. For more interesting readings on Okra and its travel worldwide, Google "origin of okra" and visit http://en.wikipedia.org/wiki/Okra.

Have you ever eaten chocolate? If yes, you've eaten African food. The cocoa that is used in your favorite chocolate comes from Ivory Coast and Nigeria. How about the tea leaves that goes into Lipton and other teas? If it is not green tea, it comes from Kenya, Cameroun and other African countries. How often are you in Starbucks getting the latte? Starbucks gets coffee in at least five African countries. Africa has great food products, even though marketed differently by U.S. companies, they are still African foods. In 2006, I was invited to speak on a panel by the Stop & Shop Supplier Diversity Director, addressing an audience of suppliers, buyers and distributors. When I told the group they ate or drank African food everyday using the examples above, they looked at me cross-eyed.

The public needs more education about the healthiness and tastiness of African Foods. Here are a few examples of healthy African foods. Many people say that Palm-Oil is high in Cholesterol. True. What people don't know is that Palm-Oil is the good Cholesterol, rich in antioxidant, trans fat free and other numerous health benefits. The Chinese now add Palm-oil to packaged foods and soaps. One of Sheba Foods' products previously mentioned was the Jute Soup which contains 210% Vitamin A and 110% Vitamin C. If you like greens (collards or kale), you will stop eating it as it is currently prepared, once you try Kenya's Sukuma Wiki or Nigerian Egusi soup. People say Egusi Soup (Sheba Foods' Melon Gourmet) is an anti-cancer dish because of all the vitamins and minerals in it.

EXPOSING CHILDREN TO AFRICAN FOODS

One of the things that prevent people from going to Africa is not knowing what is available to eat. Since I can't predict which part of the world my children will visit or reside, for their survival, I've exposed them to a variety of cuisines. A good way to educate about other cultures. If I expose them early to as many cuisines as possible, they'll not starve no matter where they are. In addition to cuisines from a number of African countries, prepared by yours truly, we enjoy various cuisines — Chinese, Italian, Caribbean, Thai and Japanese. My Lasagna is as good as, if not better than an Italian cook.

My children love the convenience of going into the freezer, taking out the frozen Jollof Rice and Sheba Stew. They add shrimp or cooked goat meat and feed themselves. I am assured that what they are eating is healthy. If they forget the cooking directions, they go to the recipe page on the Sheba Foods website and follow the directions. My 18-year old son makes light Nigerian dishes. He perfected making sushi at the age of 14. My 11 year-old daughter loves to experiment with juices and frozen smoothie combinations. I see a line of fruit juices and smoothies in Sheba Foods' future. My 7 year-old daughter is the quality assurance taster. If she likes it, all the children of the world will eat and drink it. She loves Jollof Rice. Parents who have children that are picky eaters can't believe their eyes, as those children gobble down the Jollof Rice at demos, asking for more.

I feel flattered when I hear my children boast to their friends saying: "My mother's cooking is so good, Wal-Mart bought some...." Of course there is more to getting into Wal-Mart as seen in Chapter One, than good cooking. My son, the proud Nigerian-American is off to college in the fall. He told me that the spice packets need to be part of his care package, since there is no freezer space in his dorm. He has always paid attention to what he consumed. He not only shares his Nigerian heritage with his friends, he insists on them trying the cuisines. Many of his friends and their parents now enjoy various African cuisines.

WHY IS ONLY 20% OF AFRICANS IN THE U.S. BUYING AFRICAN FOODS?

Majority of Africans in the U.S. don't buy or eat frozen dinners. Food is prepared fresh daily. A lot of African men will not eat food prepared the previous day. They want their women laboring in the kitchen every day. Most Africans purchase their African products in specialty stores called Tropical Markets. These stores offer a wide variety of African foods that Supermarkets will never stock. The Tropical Markets offer camaraderie similar to the Traditional African marketplace discussed in Chapter Six.

What happens if Supermarkets start stocking popular African products similar to those of Tropical Markets? I don't see Tropical Markets going out of business for many reasons, here is a few:

Both attract different target markets. Tropical Markets are the African immigrant's first stop in getting immigration and relocation advice. It is also the place where "Conscious" African-Americans discussed later in this Chapter, go to learn and practice African greetings. An educational center about the Motherland.

Different service. The Tropical Market clientele needs more than product, they want camaraderie. Everyone gets homesick. I go into the Tropical Markets for the familiarity of home, to mingle and get information about recent African events. While there, I can join in an ongoing conversation or start one about anything relating to home. I can't do that in Wal-Mart or any other Supermarket.

Specialty products. There are many African products that are not visually appealing and have an odor that will turn off the supermarket buyers. Yet these product are exceptionally healthy and tastes great once cooked. An example is a Nigerian product called Iru. It is fermented melon seeds and used as a soup spice. It's black in color and stinks, yet delicious once in the soups or stews. Many African Mothers' Jute soup recipe would be incomplete without it. The Sheba Foods' Jute Soup does not contain this spice for it would change the color of the soup. The nutritional value is still high despite the omission of this spice. Tropical Markets do not always educate their consumers about the African products that they stock. Many of the items have no nutritional facts and their labeling needs improvement.

When supermarkets begin stocking popular African foods, it will force the Tropical Markets to be cleaner, more organized and have competitive pricing. At the moment, there's little competition and prices are high.

DON'T SHOOT THE MESSENGER

The next two sections are not intended to make Caucasians more superior to African-Americans, nor are they intended to make African-Americans look bad. African-Americans have been through a lot living in the U.S. and still overcoming obstacles. It is common knowledge that the present U.S. history would be incomplete without African-Americans' contribution. The elevator and electricity, among other things, were inventions of African-American men.

Many people got upset at Actor Bill Cosby for speaking the truth about African-American spending habits. There is a Yoruba proverb that states: "Ti ã bá sọ otọ̀ ọrọ̀, à ku si bẹ̀; ti a bá sọ, à ku si bẹ̀" translated "We are bound to die whether or we speak the truth or not, so speak the truth." I agreed with what Mr. Cosby said, which to me was to empower African-Americans on issues that should be changed. If we don't learn from history, history will repeat itself.

There are many ethnic groups that we can learn from. One of my favorites are Jewish people. They don't sit around complaining about Holocaust. Yes, it was a major tragedy, one that the Jewish people will never let us forget. They've band together, healed and are prospering together. Why can't African-Americans and Africans do the same? As much as I want African-Americans purchasing African foods, I also ask that African-Americans purchase more African-American food products. There are many of them in non-Wal-Mart Supermarkets. Since I am in Georgia, one of my favorite places to shop is Kroger (www.kroger.com). I buy a number of African-American products there. Please take the next sections as history lessons which should not repeat themselves.

WHY ARE CAUCASIANS BUYING AFRICAN FOOD?

Demos were educational for me. African-Americans would walk past me as if I was invisible; looking at the rice and stew from the corner of their eye as they walked by. Remember, I was dressed in African garb and the table settings screamed Africa. When I felt like being a tease, I would say "come closer, I promise not to bite or I assure you there are no wild animals in the food." The question from them: "No monkey brains?" usually got a laugh and served as an ice breaker. Majority still walked by without sampling the food. Then the Caucasian curiously comes to the table without an invitation. "What is this?" they asked. "African food," I responded. He or she takes the sample and eats. If that African-American is still in the vicinity, he or she curiously looks on. Then another Caucasian steps up, a plus if with kids, eats and starts conversing with the first Caucasian as to how good the food is. They pass samples to their children, who to their surprise love it and asks for more. Suddenly, the African-American comes back and asks to try the food. It happened over and over again. It got to a point where I decided to hire a Caucasian to do the demos. Occasionally, I had one of my Caucasian friends keep my company while I did the demos.

The Sheba Foods' freezer products were in a white container (not clear). They had labels that stated "Exotic African Cuisine." The majority of the freezer buyers were Caucasians. My demo table is generally at the end of the freezer aisle where the freezer products were stocked. I would watch the Caucasian notice the product in the freezer, pick it up, read the label and put it in their pushcart. If the Caucasian decided to not buy the product, they put it back where they got it. The African-American would notice it and pick it up. As they read the part that says "Exotic African Cuisine", they dropped it like a hot potato. As soon as they walked to the next aisle, I go to the freezer and put the product where it should be.

I think Caucasians buy African foods because they are curious by nature. Or is it the African pity factor? How many African-Americans go Bundy jumping, climb mountains or go into dangerous caves to harvest antibiotics? African food purchases are perceived as adventures. One that they return to many times, for they had discovered an exciting taste.

WHY IS ONLY 2% OF AFRICAN-AMERICANS BUYING AFRICAN FOOD?

Many would argue that Caucasians have higher disposable income, and that allows them the luxury of purchasing African foods. Bill Cosby's comment leads me to believe that if African-Americans can buy $500 sneakers for themselves or their children, they can purchase African foods. More African-Americans bought the Jollof Rice in the hot deli. My guess is because it did not have a label and was seen through the glass case. I heard the Wal-Mart sales associates tell customers it was a spicy rice.   Later they told customers it was an African rice.

An unfortunate thinking that I have experienced is that when Africans are not eating themselves, they are eating wild animals.   There is no truth to this thinking.   I am told this is one of the reasons why African-Americans stay away from African foods.   I want to assure you that there are no wild animals or human flesh in any of Sheba Foods products.   As a matter of fact, most of our products start out Vegetarian, some Vegan.   Those who want protein add it.

I would love to know more reasons why African-Americans don't buy African foods.   In general, Americans are bombarded with images of starving Africans.   I will speculate that it is due to the negative African images consistently shown on television that caused many people, not just African-Americans, to distance themselves from African foods.   Maybe it is the lack of travel to the continent for a first hand experience.   Is it the shame of the slavery heritage?

The 2% of African-Americans that buy African foods are divided into two groups:

1.   Men and women married to Africans.   I was quite impressed that instead of them forcing American foods on their spouses, they sought out the African's native food or anything close to it.

2.   The other 1% is divided into three groups.

     (a)   Those who are dating the African and want to impress them, mostly women.   These were my favorites.   I felt like a match-marker.   They contacted me from all over the U.S. They conveyed the African's country, the occasion, their cooking skill level and asked for menu recommendations. Those who can't cook, place catering orders. Yes, I shipped the catering order frozen, next day delivery. Shipping costs were more than the product costs. Tells you how far one would go for their loved ones. Others got spices packets, other ingredients and cooking instructions. He watched her prepare the meal. Shortly thereafter, I am updated with the outcome. "Thank you Queen Sheba, he loved it." My response, "I hope he marries you for we need more African-Americans like you."

(b)   Those who have traveled to Africa and miss the taste. We spent at least 15 minutes reminiscing about Africa. Having them stay by the demo table drew other African-Americans.

(c)   The "Conscious" African-American. I was educated about the Conscious African-American at one of my African Dinner and Movie events. I'll discuss this group shortly.

For a very long time it bothered me that African-Americans were not buying Sheba Foods' products. I spent weeks pondering. What can I do to change this? How about a dinner where we can freely discuss African food and Africa? Create an atmosphere where all races, especially African-Americans feel comfortable in experiencing Africa. Why not add entertainment? How about a movie? Instead of movie and popcorn, let's do an African Dinner and a Movie. That's how the African Dinner and a Movie idea came to be. Each monthly event is an opportunity to "test drive" a different African country's cuisine. Whenever possible, match the cuisine to the movie's country of origin. Attendees can ask questions as to what they ate, the movie or African landscape. See Appendix One for a sample menu.

The African Dinner and a Movie idea has been well received in Atlanta with different demographics for different locations. In one place, the demographics was: 60% White and 40% African-Americans. In another place it was 100% African-Americans. I was ecstatic! I posed questions to the 100% African-American crowd:

1. Why don't they buy African foods? They said African-Americans are picky about their food and who prepares it. Their Mama told them not to eat anybody's cooking.

2. Why eat my cooking? I met most of them for the first time, meaning they didn't know me. They stated that anyone who posts a menu on their website with health benefits met their Mama's criteria. They double checked what I posted and were convinced the food would be safe.

Education is a key component of getting the African-American to taste African food. It was encouraging to know that if I show health benefits of African foods, African-Americans may buy. My desire is to host the African Dinner and a Movie worldwide. If you become one of our partners we'll post your event on our website for those in your area to attend. Join us in educating about the healthiness of African foods, culture and scenery. At the events, as I gave education and health, I gained new friends. Great fundraising concept. I'll supply the food and movie, you supply the space and audience. A good education program for U.S. Black History Month. If you have movies and menus you'll like to share, please see Appendix Two for contact information.

CONSCIOUS VERSUS UNCONSCIOUS AFRICAN-AMERICANS

I am told that there are Conscious and Unconscious African-Americans. The Conscious, also known as Pan-Africans, are well read. He or she may not have traveled to Africa, but embraces every aspect of "traditional" Africa—no Jesus. They sometimes take African names and recognize that African food is their heritage. The Conscious sees Africans and embraces them as long lost brothers or sisters as opposed to the "go back to the jungle" response I sometimes get. The Conscious refer to themselves as the Africans in America, and are likely to marry Africans. Their hair is generally kept in the natural state or braided. The Conscious is likely to buy African foods, but not in Wal-Mart. They refuse to support Wal-Mart's economy which is viewed as oppression. Where then are they buying African Foods? In Tropical Markets and on websites. We need more Conscious brothers and sisters.

The Unconscious are ashamed of their African heritage, distance themselves from Africans, and do everything possible to stay accepted in the Caucasian world. They are the ones most likely to ask about the monkey brains and huts. The Unconscious would rather vacation in Europe than in Africa. I hope this chapter speaks to those African-Americans who have not tried African foods, please try it. It is delicious.

CELEBRITY FOCUS ON AFRICA

Africa is hot on the celebrity list right now to the point where Angelina Jolie and Madonna adopted African children. Africa is also hot on African-American churches list given President Bush's incentive. President Clinton, Bono and Bill Gates put forth major African initiatives. As much as I am thrilled about Caucasian efforts, I get excited when I read or hear about African-American contribution in developing Africa.

1. Oprah's $40 million South African investment is truly commendable. This is the kind of impact Africa needs. In 20 to 30 years, those girls become women in places of power, and will transform their communities, maybe the world given this opportunity.

   Note to Oprah: You are a mother to those children. They are truly blessed to have two mothers. When they become mothers, you become a grandmother. When they tell their stories, your name will be mentioned throughout their generations. Thanks for contributing to Africa!

2. Actor Isaiah Washington traced his roots to Sierra Leone through a DNA test. His applaudable commitment in rebuilding Sierra Leone through many projects, earned him the title of Chief. It was exciting watching him do the Sierra Leonian dance at the site of the school that he is building. His effort to learn and speak his native language deserves recognition. I am sure everyone in Sierra Leone is praying for his continued success.

Note to Isaiah: Thank you for embracing your roots wholeheartedly. Please take more African-Americans with you on your next visit.

3. Actor Chris Tucker joined President Clinton and Bono on several African projects. Chris Tucker should be commended that he had been going to Africa (Soweto, Angola & Ethiopia), making contributions prior to now that Africa has become a popular destination for celebrities, churches and others.

    Note to Chris: Keep up the good work!

4. Actor Wesley Snipes is helping to develop the Nigerian movie industry. Nigeria was rated by CNN to be the third largest movie industry in the World. His experience and influence is definitely a plus in better production and monitoring of Nigerian movies.

    Note to Wesley: Thank you for helping Nigeria develop another industry for export. Have you done your DNA ancestry test? You could be a Nigerian Ibo Man.

As these celebrities own a piece of Africa, their friends and family will visit and bring back souvenirs which may include food. Food is meant to be shared. In the process of sharing with the African-Americans in the U.S., it may lead to a desire to visit Africa. Upon getting there, they discover that the images shown on television do not fully represent Africa. The misperceptions about Africa begin to fade.

WHO SHOULD BE BUYING AFRICAN FOODS?

Everybody! We need everyone of all races to assist in developing Africa. One way is by purchasing African foods, especially from companies located in Africa. Each purchase makes it possible for that business to provide employment, thereby, raising their communities' standard of living. America has a serious obesity issue. I believe that African foods are keys in getting America healthy. What do you get in return? Healthy top notch products for your entire family. It is a win-win situation.

Chapter Eight

What Now?

---

*I used to have an open mind
but my brains kept falling out.*

The last four years have been a phenomenal journey!
I survived! Thank you Ingles and Wal-Mart for the
supermarket experience. Thanks to all those God sent for a
time and season to guide and guard my steps. The Sheba
Foods story would be incomplete without thanks to my
online customers located all over the United States, with a
few outside the U.S., please keep those monthly orders
coming. I couldn't have survived without these major
catering clients who kept my cashflow out of the red — The
Africa Channel and Georgia World Congress Center.
Everyone needs to subscribe to the Africa Channel which
is on Comcast! Their educational and entertaining

programming is top notch and showcases Africa appropriately. The Africa Channel's programs are listed on their website http://www.theafricachannel.com.

I have grown to know that the food industry is not for the timid. The small profit margins make it necessary to have mega volume for survival. In bringing new products into the market, I am careful as to product packaging, pricing and placement. I've learned that selling in bulk is better, and that "private label" is a good thing. Private labeling is when I sell my product in bulk to a company, and they put their label on it. Similar to Starbucks, Lipton and chocolate companies retailing African products with no reference to their suppliers. Build a brand, sell it if an offer is made. Otherwise, it will be duplicated and one out of business. I've accepted that God blesses me with brilliant ideas, and because people are copycats, I should be flattered that my ideas are worth stealing. When I started African Dinner and a Movie in November 2006 in Atlanta, there was no one else doing it, now there are five people in Atlanta alone doing it, called something else, but the same concept.

SHEBA FOODS AT A GLANCE

The graph below summarizes Sheba Foods' infrastructure.

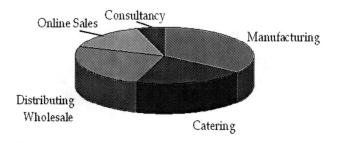

1. *Manufacturing*

    Production of products in license facilities.

2. *Distributing & Wholesale*

    Products available under our brand or other African companies' brand, for retail, food service or in bulk for private label.

3. *Catering*

    Maintaining authenticity is always my number one priority, when presenting cuisines from Algeria to Zimbabwe. Even though I prepare many African dishes, I sometimes partner with other caterers who are more familiar with the cuisine the client desires. A service we provide caterers is to broaden their offerings. By partnering with us, we provide African cuisines to complement their menus, making it seamless to their clients.

    Ethnic events especially weddings are our speciality. For example, Masai, Asanti, Yoruba, Ibo engagement parties and wedding ceremonies. Services include decor, food, customized attires and fan-fare. Our quote form can be downloaded from the catering page of our website. See Appendix One.

4. *Online orders*

    Our website handles both retail and wholesale orders. All orders are paid in full prior to shipment. Retailers can order any quantity to try in their stores. All orders are final, product exchange within 14 days of receiving product. Major supermarkets please contact us for a different arrangement.

5. *Consultancy*

Advising companies on how to get their products from concept to market. Evaluating product for necessary requirements - packaging, pricing and labeling.

Speaking engagements fall under consultancy. Please visit the speaker page for more information.

PRODUCT REFLECTIONS

It is amazing what one learns when one's survival depends on it. I started with frozen products, with minimal knowledge of the food industry. Sheba Foods strives to feature products from Algeria to Zimbabwe. I have acquired knowledge on research and development, food packaging and marketing, along with an impressive list of food contacts and buyers. Today, our various products from African countries include coffee, teas, spices, nuts, dried fruits, health juice supplements and shea butter.

Our initial products were and still are Vegetarian — Sheba Stew, Jollof Rice, Melon Gourmet and Jute Soup. The 16-ounce Sheba Stew, now comes in 1-gallon containers and spice packets. It is a rich sauce for endless uses. The 16-ounce Jollof Rice is now offered in 5-pound bags and spice packets. The Melon Gourmet and Jute Soup are generally used for catering events but also available in 1-gallon containers. The larger sizes are convenient for busy families, parties, restaurants, schools and cafeterias.

Retail: 16-ounce Sheba Stew   Wholesale/Foodservice: 1 Gallon
Dry Sheba Stew Spice available in 1-pound and 5-pound bags.

Retail: 16-ounce Sheba Stew   Wholesale/Foodservice: 5-Pounds
Dry Jollof Rice Spice available in 1-pound and 5-pound bags.

The Vegetarian products were created so the end
consumer makes it their own by adding whatever is desired.
There are recipes and videos on the Sheba Foods website to
guide unique creations.

Sheba Stew with Goat Meat   Sheba Stew with Chicken

There is nothing quick about African cuisine. It takes hours to prepare a meal. This is one of the reasons why Sheba Foods was founded - for your convenience. On our website, there are 30-minute recipes using the frozen food line. Those who prefer to do their cooking have the option of using spice packets. Two Sheba Stews were developed in response to feedback from African bachelors who desired home cooked meals. These Sheba Stews contains 3-pounds of meat — Goat Meat or Chicken. The 1-gallon container fills up a large pot, serving 8-10 people depending on how it is served. These products also offer the African wife hours of relief from the kitchen in making the stew from scratch. My hope is that African husbands see this as an opportunity to do surprise their wives with a home cooked meal. Get the Stew, cook white rice and serve. Better yet, get the Stew and 5-pound Jollof Rice, warm both up and serve. It's ready in 30-minutes to feed a family of six to eight.

There are numerous products on our website. If you don't see what you want, please let us know. We'll try to get it for you. Our special order products include green (raw) coffee, black tea and pure unrefined shea butter. For that special person, your options include:

- Gift certificates in any denomination.

- Customized gift baskets with products you specify or pick one already put together.

- Cooking classes can be conducted anywhere in the U.S., pricing will include travel expenses.

COOKING DVDs

In taking African food education to another level, I am launching cooking DVDs. There will be 17 DVDs featuring cuisines from 53 African countries. Three countries will be showcased on one DVD. The first of the series is due to be released in September 2007, featuring cuisines from Kenya, Nigeria and South Africa. My daughters helped in preparing the desert on the South African segment, shows children can prepare African cuisine. It was a lot of fun making the DVD and I hope you enjoy watching and making the recipes.

REST IN 2007

After the Wal-Mart experience, I am worn out! Sheba Foods is taking a break for 2007 from supermarket deliveries. It's time to review the four-year experience and lay a proper foundation for Sheba Foods. The saying at the beginning of Chapter 7 states: "Change your network and you'll change your net worth. My son says, make sure your net works. It's time to build a net that works, hopefully increasing the net worth.

1. Looking back on the last four years, What did I do right? Where did things go wrong?

2. Time to revamp packaging, restructure how we do business, and evaluate new products from Algeria to Zimbabwe, to represent. I hope to build African food aisles for every supermarket in the U.S. similar to the Spanish Food aisles. In preparation for that initiative I am working on a Food Tradeshow, Flavors of Africa, planned for Nigeria.

   For more information see Appendix Three or visit ww.flavorsofafrica.com/abuja2007.asp.

4. Time to find a mentor or mentors.

5. Build a team of sales representatives.

Until my re-entry in 2008, your options for our gourmet products are: Catering, Online orders and African Dinner and Movie events. Thank you for allowing me to share my story with you.

It is well with your soul and mine!

We are Blessed and highly favored.

Appendices

Why is it when we talk to God we're praying,
but when God talks to us, we're schizophrenic?"
Lily Tomlin

Appendix One

Download our quote form at
http://www.shebafoods.com/catering.htm
Email questions to: orders@shebafoods.com

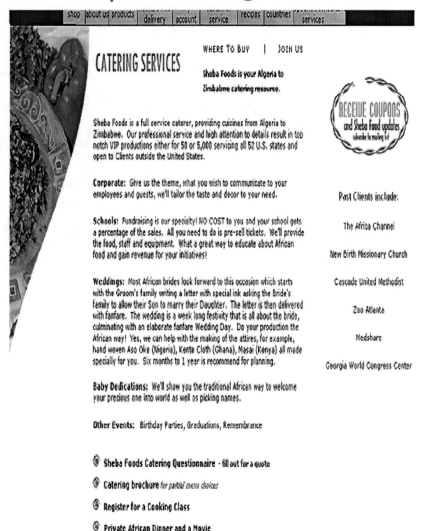

shop | about us | products | delivery | account | service | recipes | countries | services

CATERING SERVICES

WHERE TO BUY | JOIN US

Sheba Foods is your Algeria to Zimbabwe catering resource.

RECEIVE COUPONS and Sheba food updates

Sheba Foods is a full service caterer, providing cuisines from Algeria to Zimbabwe. Our professional service and high attention to details result in top notch VIP productions either for 50 or 5,000 servicing all 52 U.S. states and open to Clients outside the United States.

Corporate: Give us the theme, what you wish to communicate to your employees and guests, we'll tailor the taste and decor to your need.

Schools: Fundraising is our specialty! NO COST to you and your school gets a percentage of the sales. All you need to do is pre-sell tickets. We'll provide the food, staff and equipment. What a great way to educate about African food and gain revenue for your initiatives!

Weddings: Most African brides look forward to this occasion which starts with the Groom's family writing a letter with special ink asking the Bride's family to allow their Son to marry their Daughter. The letter is then delivered with fanfare. The wedding is a week long festivity that is all about the bride, culminating with an elaborate fanfare Wedding Day. Do your production the African way! Yes, we can help with the making of the attires, for example, hand woven Aso Oke (Nigeria), Kente Cloth (Ghana), Masai (Kenya) all made specially for you. Six months to 1 year is recommend for planning.

Baby Dedications: We'll show you the traditional African way to welcome your precious one into world as well as picking names.

Other Events: Birthday Parties, Graduations, Remembrance

Past Clients include:

The Africa Channel

New Birth Missionary Church

Cascade United Methodist

Zoo Atlanta

Medshare

Georgia World Congress Center

- Sheba Foods Catering Questionnaire - fill out for a quote
- Catering brochure for partial menu choices
- Register for a Cooking Class
- Private African Dinner and a Movie
- Email us: info@shebafoods.com

Call us today!!!

Appendix One

A Sample 3-Course Nigerian (West African) Menu with Vegetarian and Meat options.

	NON-VEGETARIAN	VEGETARIAN (VEGAN)
APPETIZER:	**Akara - Bean Cakes** *Nigerian Red Beans, Onions, Eggs, Spices & Oil* High in Protein	
ENTREE:	**Tilapia in Sheba Stew, Jollof Rice, Fried Plantains** *Tilapia, Stew & Rice contains Tomatoes, Onions, Ginger, Garlic, Curry & other Spices, Plantains & Oil*	**Tofu in Sheba Stew, Jollof Rice, Fried Plantains** *Tofu, Stew & Rice Tomatoes, Onions, Ginger, Garlic, Curry & other Spices, Plantains & Oil*
	-- Tilapia is a great source of Protein, Phosphorus, Niacin, Vitamin B12 and Selenium. -- Sheba Stew high in nutrients with antioxidants and minerals from the tomatoes, onions and spices. -- Jollof Rice A good source of insoluble fiber rich in spices. Among other nutrients, rice is rich in carbohydrates, the main sources of energy, low in fat, contains some protein and plenty of B vitamins. -- Plantains is high in potassium -- Tofu is a highly nutritious, protein-rich food that is made from the curds of soybean milk.	
DESERT:	**Dried Mangoes & Pineapples** *Mangoes & Pineapples*	

Appendix Two

Come, eat, network and watch great African movies! African Dinner and a Movie is a FUN educational tool in learning about African food, culture and scenery. We hope to remove misperceptions and/or stereotypes with the discussions that follow each screening.

Hosted by Adonai Foundation, Inc. a non-profit foundation, so your tickets are tax deductible. Join us by hosting an event in your city and list it on our site. Movie, Menu and Event details are available on the website.

For Menu, Movie and Event Details, visit
www.africandinnerandamovie.com

Appendix Two

Please visit www.africandinnerandamovie.com
for Menu, Movie, Locations and Event details.

Appendix Three

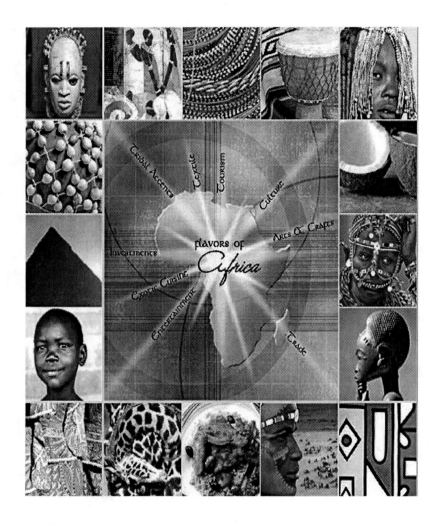

Please visit www.flavorsofafrica.com for more details.

hosted by a non-profit foundation

Appendix Three

FLAVORS OF *Africa*

   Flavors of Africa is a bold attempt to demystify Africa and build cultural, technical and investment bridges between Africa and America.

   Strategic alliances with African governments, NGOs and business organizations are being formed to raise public awareness of the event and marketplace. We are looking for progressive companies and people to partner in our vision.

   Please visit http://www.flavorsofafrica.com for dates, locations of an event and registration details. Your financial support of Flavors of Africa is critical to its success. Sponsors and Exhibitors have a unique diversity investment opportunity to expose their products and/or services to various ethnicities.

   Be a Sponsor, Exhibitor, Attendee or Volunteer. We look forward to your partnership.

Buyers: Travel expenses are reimburseable depending on volume of product purchase from event. Buyer's questionnaire downloadable on website.

Exhibitors: Download questionnaire and registration forms on the website.

Sponsors: Email us at sponsor@flavorsofafrica.com for more information

Mailing address: Please visit website for mailing address. Georgia, U.S.A.

Appendix Four

Appendix Four

Exotic African Cuisines made simple by Kunmi Oluleye, author of *Life with Wal-Mart: A Vendor's Story* and *Selling My Food To Supermarkets, Distributors, Etc.*. This DVD is entertaining as well as educative. There are trivia questions to reveal the African country's cuisine to be prepared. Kunmi takes you shopping for ingredients at various locations, prior to cooking in the kitchen. Get Step-by-Step cooking instructions and Nutrition information on various Foods.

A great video for all ages. This is the first of 17 DVD series featuring mouth-watering recipes. This DVD focuses on Kenya, Nigeria and South Africa. Watch Kunmi's daughters ages 7 & 11 help with the cooking in the South African segment. No prior African or any other type of cooking experience required. An educational gift for anyone!

Kenyan Menu: Macadamian Nuts, Sukuma Wiki, Ugali, Goat Meat and Mandaazi

Nigerian Menu: Nigerian Salad, Tilapia in Sheba Stew, Plantains, Jollof Rice, Vegetables & Shrimp and Fruit Medley

South Africa Menu: Green Bean Salad, Cape Kidgeree (Rice & Fish) and Custard Strawberry Banana Pudding

Host / Executive Producer:	Kunmi Oluleye
Format:	Color, DVD-Video, NTSC
Language:	English
Number of discs:	1 — One
Rating:	Not Rated
Run Time:	110 minutes

Appendix Five

Appendix Five

Just think, Ready-to-eat authentic African cuisine retailing in major supermarkets? Sheba food has made this a reality. This is a story of how an African woman crossed various barriers: cultural, race, gender, faith and issues of being a small business.

An easy to follow, strongly recommended guide on issues in getting one's food or product to market. Come along on the author's journey on getting her ethnic cuisines into major supermarkets and other retailers. This book tells all. It shows pitfalls, and offers help at potential crossroads. The book is full of illustrations, questions to guide your thoughts and decision. This well written guide is a must for anyone who has a product that should be sold to the public.

Book is available in Paperback and PDF on www.amazon.com

Paperback:	188 pages
Number of Chapters:	Nine
Publisher:	IROK Solutions, Inc.
Publication Date:	October 31, 2004
Language:	English
ISBN-10:	0965480100
ISBN-13:	978-0965480109
Product Dimensions:	9 x 6 x 0.5 inches
Shipping Weight:	9.8 ounces

Appendix Six

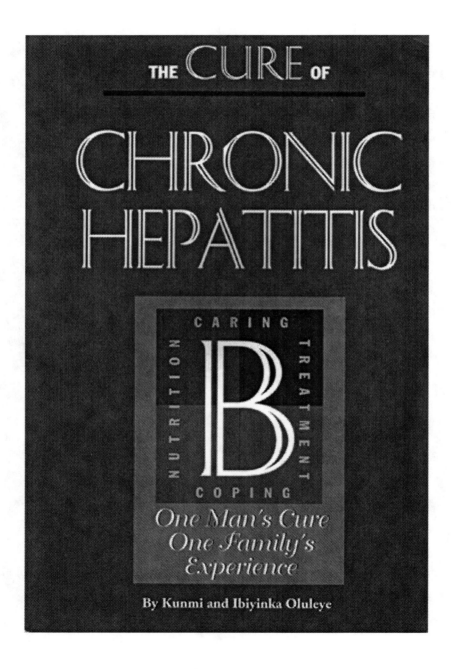

THE CURE OF

CHRONIC HEPATITIS

NUTRITION
CARING
TREATMENT
COPING

B

*One Man's Cure
One Family's
Experience*

By Kunmi and Ibiyinka Oluleye

Appendix Six

This is a source of detailed information of the treatment of a Hepatitis B patient. Even though the focus is on Hepatitis B, there's useful information and resources listed for other hepatitis types, especially Hepatitis C.

The book is written in journal form to give the readers a complete picture of the authors' experience. Read about the six-month combination treatment of Interferon Alpha-2b and Ribavirin (Virazole). There are tables clearly listing drugs, food intakes, vitamins and homones. A great resource for anyone associated with hepatitis directly or indirectly, every victim, family or friend, hepatologist, nurse or medical student. Be informed about this deadly disease.

Book is available in Paperback on www.amazon.com

Paperback:	187 pages
Number of Chapters:	Nine
Publisher:	IROK Solutions, Inc.
Publication Date:	January 1997
Language:	English
ISBN-10:	0965480194
ISBN-13:	978-0965480192
Product Dimensions:	8.5 x 5.5 x 0.5 inches
Shipping Weight:	9.6 ounces

Appendix Seven

Exotic Vacations

 Sheba Travel

You've come to the right place for lowest custom travel fares. Thanks for the oppoturnity to quote your travel.

Travel Packages available for:

Africa

Caribbean

Europe

South America

 ENTER SITE

Appendix Seven

Specializing in Group Travel to numerous locationsbe it trade exploration, church missions or family reunions. We are here to make your travel pain free and memorable.

SERVICES WE PROVIDE:

- Air, Hotel, Ground Transportation and Meals
- Travel documents and insurance (Visa experditing)
- Tailored itineraries
- Tour package for many budgets
- Tour Packages with Tour Guides
- Honeymoon Packages
- Golf Excursions
- Safari Packages

Please visit us at www.shebatravel.com

BACK TO YOUR ROOTS TRAVEL BEGINS SOON!

Africa is our specialty.   Join us on the Back To Your Roots Travel which combines trade exploration with vacation or church mission. A different country every month.

For more information please visit
www.backtoyourroots.com for more details.

Email us at info@shebatravel.com for a quote!

Notes

page intentionally left blank

GLOSSARY

Invoice Factoring - a funding method where finance companies buy invoices, charging a percentage of the amount.

Demo - short for demonstrate. A marketing alternative for suppliers in promoting their products.

Store Planogram - the layout of the stores shelves showing product placement. This is how buyers communicate with department managers about new products placement. Planograms change per category cycle.

Category Management - a process used in the food industry to manage product categories as strategic business units, producing enhanced business results by focusing on delivering consumer value.

Local Supplier Questionnaire (LSQ) - form for minority companies who desire to put their products in Wal-Mart.

Food Merchandiser (FM) - personnel who oversee food products in all categories for multiple stores.

Direct Store Delivery (DSD) - delivery to each store by supplier who hires the staff and transportation needed.

Jambalaya - a rice, meat and vegetable dish native to Louisiana, New Orleans, U.S.A. Variation of the West African Jollof Rice.

Paella - a rice, meat, seafood and vegetable dish native to Spain. Variation of the West African Jollof Rice.

Slotting fees - is a fee charged to food companies to have their product placed on supermarket shelves. The fee varies greatly depending on the product and market conditions. For a new product, the initial slotting fee may be $25,000 per item in a regional cluster of stores, but may be as high as $250,000 in high-demand markets. *Source: http://en.wikipedia.org/wiki/Slotting_fee*

Co-packer - also known as contract packaging, a widely used option of having a company with the proper equipment and setup produce and package one's product(s).

Home store - refers to the store a food merchandiser or district manager is likely to be found.

Dun & Bradstreet Supplier Evaluation Report - a report Wal-Mart generated by Dun & Bradstreet that show companies credit worthiness.

Bible Belt - generally used to describe Georgia and other states or cities where majority of the population attend church.

Reference

Yoruba Resources

For those who want to learn more about the Yoruba culture and language.

Dr. Adebusola Onabajo Onayemi

Dr. Onayemi, a Yoruba man, with assistance from Mr. James Kass developed a Yoruba font. To download the Yoruba font, see visuals, hear pronunciations of the alphabets and more information on the Yoruba language, please visit http://www.learnyoruba.com.

Dr. Pamela Smith

Dr. Smith is a Professor at the University of Nebraska, Omaha, where she teaches English, Humanities and Women's Studies courses. She has won numerous awards for research and teaching, including the 1994 Excellence in teaching Award at the University of Nebraska, Omaha. Her publications include: Tongue and Mother Tongue (co-edited, Africa World Press, 2002); English translations of Akínwùmí Ìsolá's Efúnsetán Aníwúrà, Ìyálóde Ibadan & Tinúubú, Ìyálóde Egbá (Africa World Press, 2005) from Yorùbá. She is presently translating Adébáyo Fáléti's revolutionary novel, Omo Olókùn-esin into English. Her work-in-progress on the Yorùbá language and cultural studies with colleague, Dr. Onàyemí, can be found at www.yorubadictionary.com.

Other Resources

1.   Wal-Mart Website http://www.walmart.com

2.   Wake-up Wal-Mart Website
     http://www.wakeupwalmart.com

3.   *Wal-Mart: The High Cost of Low Price* by Robert Greenwald.
     BraveNewFilms available on amazon.com ASIN: B000BTH4K4
     http://www.walmartmovie.com

4.   *The Man who said No to Wal-Mart* by Charles Fishman Excerpt
     from book *Wal-Mart Effects* by Charles Fishman, The Penguin
     Press, December 26, 2006, ISBN-10: 0143038788.

5.   Wikipedia Website has numerous articles and Wal-Mart Facts
     which includes percentage of females in Wal-Mart's management,
     court cases, environmental and employment violations.
     http://en.wikipedia.org/wiki/Wal-Mart

6.   *Dukes v. Wal-Mart Stores, Inc.* is the discrimination case by
     Attorney Brad Seligman.
     http://en.wikipedia.org/wiki/Dukes_v._Wal-rt_Stores%2C_Inc.

7.   *Is Wal-Mart Hostile to Women?* By Conlin, Michelle. Business
     Week. July 16, 2001.
     http://www.businessweek.com/magazine/content/01_29/
     b3741080.htm

8.   *No Way to Treat a Lady?* by Wendy Zellner, Business Week.
     March 3, 2003.
     http://www.businessweek.com/magazine/content/03_09/b38220
     67_mz021.htm

9.   *Wal-Mart Faces Class-Action Lawsuit.* Associated Press.
     February 6, 2007.
     http://newsmax.com/archives/articles/2007/2/6/130433.shtml

10. *Wal-Mart to appeal discrimination suit status* by Staff Writer,
     CNNMoney.com, February 6, 2007.
     http://money.cnn.com/2007/ 02/06/news/companies/
     walmart/?postversion=2007020617

11. *Jesse Jackson Exposed* by Chris Arabia, FrontPageMagazine.com December 9, 2002, http://www.frontpagemag.com/Articles/ReadArticle.asp?ID= 4986

12. *Shakedown: Exposing the Real Jesse Jackson* by Kenneth Timmerman, Regnery Publishing, Inc., March 4, 2002, ISBN-10: 0895261650

13. *The Next Big (Legal) Thing?* by Chuck Salter, Fast Company, Issue 69, March 2003, Page 112 http://www.fastcompany.com/magazine/69/nextbigthing.html

14. *Firing Back At The Beast* by Jonathan Tasini on Working Life Friday 25 of May, 2007. http://www.workinglife.org/blogs/view_post.php?content_id=651 4#comment_6517

15. *With Profits Elusive, Wal-Mart to Exit Germany*, by Ann Zimmerman and Emily Nelson. Other contributors to the article: Deborah Ball and Kris Hudson. *Wall Street Journal*, July 29, 2006.

16. *Wal-Mart's Germany Exit Reflects on Its Market Entry Strategy* by John Davison and Mim Burt http://www.gartner.com/DisplayDocument?doc_cd=142370

17. *Wal-Mart Finds Dominance Harder to Achieve in Europe,* By John Davison and Stephen Smith *Gartner Research Publication* 2 August 2006, ID Number: G00142370 P. 89

18. *Development Policy Review* by Dave D. Weatherspoon and Thomas Reardon, 2003, May, 21 (3) The Rise of Supermarkets in Africa: Implications for Agrifood Systems and the Rural Poor.

19. *Retail sales surged in November, but ...* by Parija B. Kavilanz, CNNMoney.com staff writer, December 13 2006 http://money.cnn.com/2006/12/13/news/economy/retail_sales/ index.htm

Index

3 1170 00783 7085

Printed in the United States
92735LV00001B/1-48/A